. . . If anyone is in Christ, he is a new creation; old things have passed away; behold all things have become new...

(NKJV) 2nd Corinthians 5:17

The Man I Was

A Life
Changed
Blessed
And Used
By God

The True Story of
Dave Tripiciano

Two Harbors Press
212 3rd Avenue North, Suite 290
Minneapolis, MN 55401
612.455.2293
www.TwoHarborsPress.com

ISBN-13: 978-1-937928-93-3
LCCN: 2012938798

Distributed by Itasca Books

Cover Design by Sophie Chi
Typeset by James Arneson

Printed in the United States of America

DEDICATION

To My Wife And Best Friend Mary

Thank you for loving me when I'm at my best and at my worst.
Thank you for having the patience and the wisdom to let me
spend huge blocks of time writing and editing,
because you knew that this story had to be told.
You are a beautiful, strong, godly woman
and I'm very blessed to have you.

THANK YOU

To My Lord And Savior Jesus Christ

Thank you for saving me, blessing me beyond
my wildest dreams and using me.
Thank you Lord, for changing me from the man I was,
into the man that I am today.

A SINCERE APOLOGY

To All The People I Hurt, Wronged And Disappointed

My most heartfelt and sincere apology to all of the people, living and deceased, that I hurt, disappointed and deserted as a self centered young man leading a life of sin. Two of my greatest wishes are that you will someday understand and forgive me; and that I could somehow go back in time and do many things differently, knowing what I know now.

ABOUT THIS BOOK

Dear Friend:

The story you are about to read is not an easy one for me to tell, but I feel compelled to tell it, so that many might be encouraged by how real God has been in my life. He has changed me, blessed me, and used my gifts to encourage, teach and bless others; in spite of the self centered, sinful life I led as a young man. This tragic, yet victorious true story was also dramatized, and used as an episode of the well known, classic Christian radio program "Unshackled". It was broadcast around the world in March of 2011.

I wrote this detailed account of my life, for a Hollywood competition that was looking for an original screenplay, with a spiritually uplifting Christian message, because I believe it would make a very touching movie. Since it's written in screenplay format; you will need to use your imagination to "see" the scenes unfolding on the screen. Sometimes I have a series of short scenes with no dialogue, designed to have just musical background, and "Dave's" voice as a narrator telling the story. In that case, the narrator's part for the scene is shown first, and then the scene is described in detail right below.

To make this long, complex story shorter and easier to tell; some minor details have been left out, modified, or rearranged slightly. This also helps make this true account more suitable for a movie or a book.

At the time of this writing, I have many pre-teen students who love, respect and look up to me. I urge parents <u>not</u> to allow their children to read this book, until they can preview it first. Some segments show me as a college student and young adult, playing in bands and womanizing; so it may not be appropriate for young children and especially my students.

Thank you for taking the time to read this book. I hope you will enjoy it, be encouraged by it, and tell as many people as you can about it.

In His Service:

Dave Tripiciano

SPONSORS AND SUPPORTERS

I would like to thank the following people, businesses and organizations that made this book possible with financial donations or photography. I would also like to thank all of the parents who graciously allowed me to use their child's image in one of the photos that enhance this book.

Todd & Lora Walter

Joe Vitale

Judy Murray

Bryan & Tamara Albert

Todd & Amy Murray

John & Sue Kelly

Diane Temple

Wade & Cindy Dalton

James & Sandra Cole

The Rodriguez Family

Scott & Michelle McNaughton

Five Star Home Improvements

Geneseo Assembly Of God Church

Other Anonymous Donors

Several Of The Photographs Were Taken By:
Richard Meredith III
Kevin Gundel

CONTENTS

THE GYM FLOOR
MUST BE DRY-
MOPPED AFTER
EACH USE

Act 1 •
The Job Interview Arranged by God

A small classroom in an older school building:

The poorly lit, narrow room is way too small and the wrong shape to be a band room, yet it's set up with folding chairs, mismatched music stands, instrument cases, a dented tuba, and a couple of old, well-worn drums. In one corner, there is a man working earnestly at a large, heavy, discolored desk. He appears to be in his early forties, with dark hair, a slight build, and a dark goatee. Behind him, through the classroom door on the far side of the room, a shy, pretty, wholesome-looking high-school girl with red hair and freckles enters the room. The man is unaware that she is there. She begins to quietly arrange the chairs and music stands. She inadvertently tips over a music stand, which lands on the floor with a loud clang, startling the teacher and causing him to turn to see her standing there.

Dave
[Surprised]
Hey! What're you doin' here, Betsy?

Betsy
Oh nuthin', I had a free period, so I thought I'd come down and help you set up for band practice.

Dave

[Chuckling Softly]

Wow! [**pauses**] You gave up your free period and came to help me, without being asked?

Betsy

[Shrugging, as she moves a chair]

Study hall's pretty boring, and I actually look forward to band practice since you came. The band's gettin' bigger and we're starting to sound really good!

Dave

[His face softens - he is pleased and deeply touched]

I never thought I'd say this, [smiles] but I've been looking forward to band practice quite a bit myself. We really are starting to sound good, and I get to work with a lot of great kids, like you. **[He picks up a music stand and begins to help her]**

Betsy

[With excitement, as they work]

Do you really think we might be able to get those old uniforms from Geneseo? It's hard to believe they're really blue and white. If we get 'em it will be the first time we've ever had real band uniforms; and they'll be in our school colors!

Dave

Well, it looks like we might. The band director said we could have 'em if we want 'em. But they're pretty old and musty, and they've been in a closet since the '70s. We'll have to get them dry-cleaned and get some of the moms to have a sewing bee to spiff them up.

Betsy

[Eagerly]

Were you serious when you said we might march in a parade in the spring? I'm pretty excited about that.

Dave

Well if the band keeps growing, I don't see why we can't. It would be a great experience for you guys, and playing Christian music out on the streets would be a powerful ministry and a really unique way to touch lives for Christ. You've got a servant's heart, Betsy. Since you're a good musician, and all the kids look up to you, maybe I'll pick you to be the drum major and student director to lead the band down the street in parades?

Betsy

[A look of shock, awe, and disbelief gives way to a smile]

That would be amazing! I'd be proud to do it, and happy to help with something that important. You could count on me to give my best for the band, Mr. Trip.

Dave

I know you would, Betsy, that's why I thought of you for the job.

Betsy

[Blushes, nods, and then looks at the floor as they continue to work]

Dave

[We hear his thoughts]

What a great kid, I can't believe there are still kids this wholesome and this nice in America today.

I wasn't even looking for a job, but God put me here, where he could use my gifts and experience. I took the job to bless a small Christian school, but I'm the one that's being blessed beyond my wildest dreams!

Betsy
How many chairs and music stands do you want in the top row, where the trumpets and trombones sit?

Dave
I think we need seven chairs and four stands there, but we'll make sure as people come in.
[Fade to black]

Five months earlier: Dave, his wife Mary, and their daughter Nicole are seated in the principal's office of the school in three chairs facing his desk. Nicole is seated to the far right [back stage]. Behind the desk sits Ron Davis the school principal, a tall, big boned older man with thick glasses and gray hair. He is smiling as he speaks to the three of them in loud booming tones.

Ron Davis
[Smiling broadly]
Well, Nicole, welcome to Lima Christian School. You seem like a very nice young lady. I know you're going to like it here as much as we're going to like having you as one of our students.
[pauses, then looks at Dave] How about you Dave, what do you do for a living?

Dave
Well, I've filmed and produced several hunting and wildlife videos that have a Christian message. I sell them at outdoor shows and I'm a guest speaker for hunter's outreach dinners. I give hunting seminars and share a salvation message with the men at those events.
[pauses, nods; then looks off before continuing on, slowly and quietly] But before we lost Nicole's mother in a car accident, I was a school band director for twenty years.

[An awkward silence. A tear drips down Nicole's cheek]
Mary also lost her husband—in a plane crash—when her children were little, but God arranged for us to meet; and He brought the two of us, and our five children, together. The Bible says that all things work together for good for those who love the Lord and are called according to his purposes, and that has definetly been true for us. He used unspeakable tragedies to bring us together, change us, redirect our lives, and use us. As a result of Cecelia's death, insurance paid off my mortgage; Mary also has income and benefits due to the tragic loss of her husband. That put us in a financial position where I could leave teaching and start a ministry for sportsmen, and Mary could be at home for the kids, at least for now while they're young.

Ron Davis
[Quite shocked, his eyes widen with surprise. He works hard to respond respectfully to this tragic news and also contain his eagerness and excitement as he learns that Dave is an experienced band director]

Oh no, I'm so sorry. I'm so very sorry to hear that. You guys seem like such a close-knit, happy family; it would've been hard for me to guess that just talking to you. **[pauses, looks at Mary]** How about you Mary, what do you do?

Mary
I'm a registered nurse with a bachelor's degree in nursing. When the kids were little, I worked in hospitals, the college health center, and a hospice home, but for now I'm a mom and a wife.

Ron Davis
[Slowly, thoughtfully]
Wow . . . you do have an amazing story. Only God could allow so much good to come out of such terrible tragedies. I see His hand all over you guys, opening up new chapters in your lives, sending you in different directions, and using your gifts in new and exciting ways.

[Pauses, then speaks intently and passionately directly to Dave and Mary] But now that you tell me all that, I know that it's no accident that the two of you are sitting in my office today.

[Smiling, he tactfully switches gears, speaking with a growing sense of eagerness and excitement] I believe it's for a much bigger reason than just enrolling Nicole in our school, and I believe God is about to send your lives down yet another path, to use you in a way you never expected! **[To Dave]** Were you really a school band director for twenty years? High school or elementary, and what school district did you work for?

Dave
Grades four through twelve, in three different districts around the state. **[pauses]** My marching bands have played for the Buffalo Bills and won a state championship, but after the accident I just didn't have the heart to do it anymore.

Ron Davis
[To Dave] Our band director just left in the spring. **[Shaking his head with disappointment]** She was the kind of teacher that made band really boring and turned most of the kids off. I think there were only eight or nine kids in the band when she left.

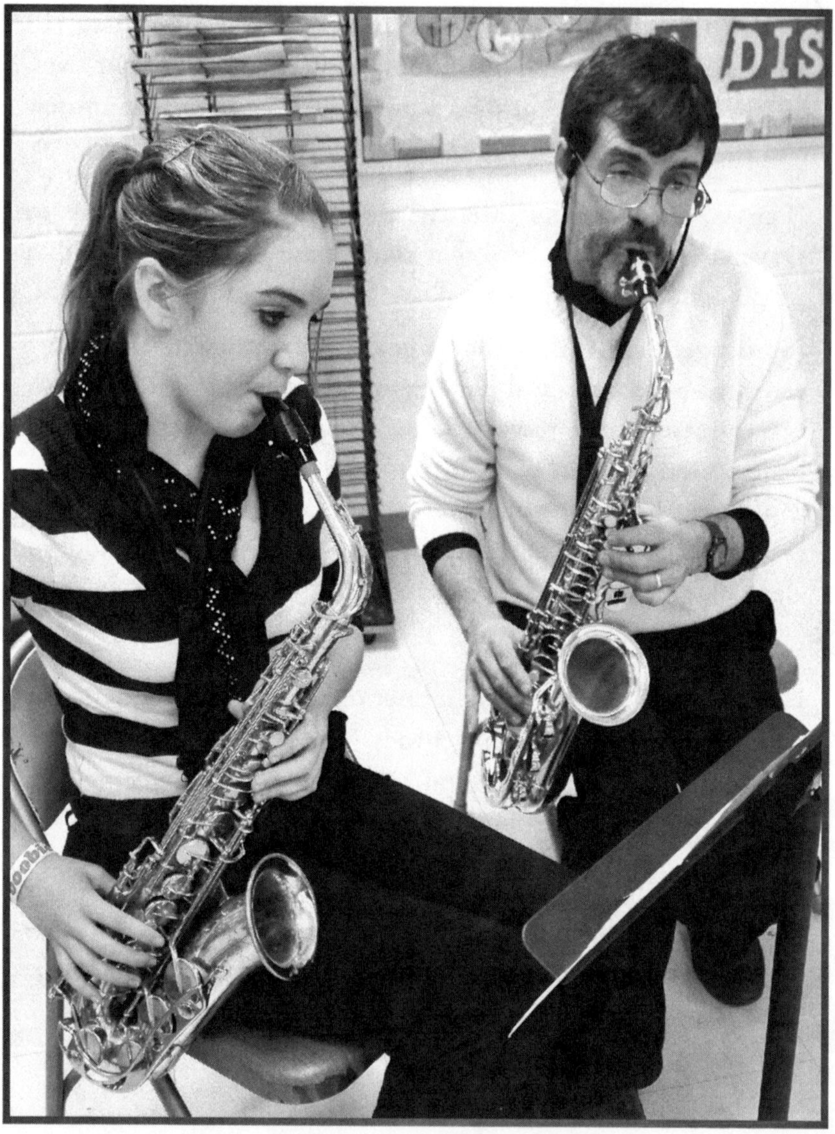

[pauses again, then points his finger at Dave with great weight and urgency] We've been praying all summer that God would send us a band director, Dave, and I believe that you sitting here in my office two weeks before school starts is God's answer to that prayer!

Dave
[Stunned and speechless]

Ron Davis
[Excited and urgently, like a high-pressure salesman]
Would you ever consider going back into teaching and becoming our band director? What a blessing it would be to have someone with all of your experience here to work with our kids! We don't pay a lot, but you'd be giving your time and talents to an important ministry and you'd get to work with some of the greatest kids in the world! What do you say, Dave? We'd be thrilled to have you, and I know the kids and parents would love working with you!

Dave
[Taken off guard, he is nervous and apologetic as he tries to think of every excuse to gracefully get out of taking the job]
Whoa, this is quite a surprise! Wow, I'm very flattered! Very, very flattered. **[pauses]**

[Chuckles, then smiles] Actually, it would be kind of fun, but at this point in my life, I'm not really sure I'd ever want to go back into teaching band and instrumental music.

Ron
[Nods with understanding (and disappointment), as Dave continues]

Dave

God has given me an important ministry to men, speaking and sharing my videos with them. I'm actually still in the process of filming and finishing a couple of videos and it's very time-consuming work. I'm also gone a lot, traveling for speaking engagements, filming animals, hunting, and selling my videos at outdoor shows. After having that kind of freedom and making a living doing something I love, it would be pretty hard to go back to the grind of coming to school every day and listening to kids (who never practice) play wrong notes. **[pauses, then tries to make a joke to lighten the mood]** Besides, Ron, every band teacher knows that nothing's scarier than an E-flat alto saxophone in the hands of a fourth grader!

Nicole

[Smiles, shaking her head]

Ron and Mary

[Smile and nod]

Ron Davis

[Disappointed by Dave's initial response, but not giving up]

Well, band only meets every other day; we could make it a part-time position and you could work on your videos on the off-days. If you have to travel to film, speak, hunt, or be at an outdoor show—go ahead. We'll work around your schedule and your ministry. It would be worth it just to get a band teacher with your experience and your background in here to work with our kids!

[pauses]

[Smiles as he moves his gaze from one face to the next] Are you guys beginning to suspect that God is up to something here? Is anyone else other than me convinced that it's his plan that you're sitting in my office today? If you don't believe that yet, then the next thing I tell you will prove it to you for sure!

[pauses and points at Mary with a big smile, speaking very slowly] We also need a school nurse very badly, right now! **[pauses]** Our nurses have been volunteers in the past, but if you'll take the job, Mary, and convince your husband to take over the band, we'll find a way to pay you as much as we can. Now, if all that isn't enough, I'm also happy to tell you that with both of you working here, Nicole would then be able to attend our school tuition-free.

Mary
[Smiling and nodding eagerly]
Wow! I might really enjoy doing that now that the kids are getting older. If we take the jobs and the tuition's covered, maybe we'll have our three younger ones come to school here too! Then we can all ride together every morning. I think you're right, Mr. Davis, God is definitely at work here today.

Dave
[Dave sits speechless, slowly shaking his head. He is stunned, surprised, pleased, and in awe of everything he has just heard]

[Softening, he shakes his head and smiles]
You're right, hun. I hate to admit it, but I almost have to believe God is trying to tell us something. **[pauses]**

[To Ron Davis] You're a great principal, a very wise man, and you drive a hard bargain, Ron. You just took away all of my excuses for not taking the job in one sentence; and then in the next one you offered my wife a job and our kids free tuition.

[pauses, nodding; deep in thought as he tries to process everything]

When I walked into this room today the last thing I wanted to do was go back into teaching, but it sure looks like God might have other plans and a different use for me than I thought. We'll go home and pray about it, and then we'll call you back. Can we have a couple of days to think about it?

Ron
[elatedly, jumping up to shake hands]
Absolutely! Take until the weekend. I'll be looking forward to your call. It would be great to have all three of you here, and a big blessing for our school.

[Fade to black]

A couple of days later, Dave is in his back yard. It is a spacious, narrow yet deep yard. Secluded and fairly private, it's surrounded by trees and brush. Farmland is on two sides of the property and a similar large yard is on the third side. From the back yard, there's only one other house visible (other than Dave and Mary's at a distance). There's an old wooden swing in the center of the yard; that looks like it hasn't been used in quite a while. Dave is seated alone on the worn-out swing. He's deep in thought, staring at the ground and then off into the brush and sky as he talks to himself, talks and listens to God, and prays.

Dave

[aloud, with concern and thoughtfulness]

It really looks like this is your hand at work, Father. You set up a job interview for Mary and I, and we weren't even looking for a job. **[long pause]**

[new idea] The principal said there are only eight or nine kids in the band. What am I supposed to do with that? What if they're all flutes? Or, worse yet, drummers? **[makes a face]**

Dave stops talking aloud and we hear his thoughts. His sentences are being phrased as though someone else is speaking to him. His inner tone is suddenly gentle, loving, and encouraging, and his attitude is very different. It's as if God is speaking through him and to him in his own voice, giving him encouraging thoughts and words to reassure him and guide his decision.

Dave

[His thoughts, hearing a "God-inspired" voice]

It might start out small, but you could build it up. You know what you've done with bands in other schools. Maybe you could march in parades, playing Christian music on the public streets. That would be a great ministry and a wonderful way to touch more lives. **[pauses, contemplates]** *It's true: a lot more people go to parades than hunter's dinners.*

[Nods, pauses thoughtfully, then continues]

The school mascot name is the Saints. You could call the band the "Marching Saints" and you could write an arrangement of "When The Saints Go Marchin' In" to be your theme song. . . .

[looks skyward, then into the brush; then the inner voice goes on] *Do you remember the things that you said, and the prayer that you prayed that night in the woods a few days after Cecelia's death?*

As Dave stares off into the brush thoughtfully, we see into his face and then his eyes. The screen becomes misty and dreamlike as the scene fogs, fades, and then begins to clear on a completely different scene that is etched forever in his mind. The time is four years earlier and we are seeing a flashback from his memory: Dave is standing alone on a country road in the pouring rain. He is near the edge of the pavement, in a spot where the road has a sharp bend, on a steep, downhill grade. The culvert is plugged and water is flowing across the road, causing bad flooding in this low spot. His dripping wet face has an expression of shock and disbelief as he looks into the woods.

Behind him, and pulled over to the opposite shoulder, is his car, engulfed by a small river of rainwater that swirls around the tires. The rain-washed vehicle is still running, with its lights on and the wipers beating. We see the dark silhouettes of his three children inside, pressed against the fogged-up windows and peering out in the direction of their father as he moves along the far shoulder toward the tragic scene in the woods.

Ten paces into the woods his wife's car lays mangled and twisted in the trees. A path of small saplings, which have been shorn off and splintered, leads his eyes to the wrecked car, which has come to rest with its front end wrapped around a tree and its roof flattened and caved in. Many handfuls of broken glass scattered across the hood are all that remain of what was once the front windshield, and the front passenger side door is wide open.

As Dave approaches the vehicle, he sees his wife, Cecelia, lying on her back on the front seat, with her head toward the steering wheel and her feet sticking out of the open door. Her shoeless feet are black and blue, and she is making gurgling sounds from her mouth and chest as she tries to breath.

[Dave's memory jumps ahead in time]
He is sitting alone in a small hospital waiting room, staring sullenly at the floor and shaking his head sadly as a young male doctor and two nurses come in.

Young Doctor
Mr. Tripiciano?

Dave
[looking up anxiously]
Yes?

Young Doctor
[slowly, with sympathy]
Your wife's head and internal injuries were quite extensive.

[Dramatic pause]

We did everything we possibly could, but we couldn't save her. We're very sorry for your loss. If we could have flown her to the major trauma center in Sayre, she might have had a chance. But it's raining so hard they couldn't land the Mercy Flight chopper.

Dave
[yelling, frantically]
No! Keep trying! You've got to keep trying! You can bring her back! Please don't give up—we have three children!

[Breaks down, sobbing uncontrollably]
This stuff always happens on the eleven o'clock news to other people, but it's not supposed to happen to you in real life.

[One of the nurses puts a comforting hand on Dave's shoulder]

Young Doctor
[patiently]
Once again, we are very, very sorry for your loss, but we really did everything humanly and medically possible to save her.

[Another quick cut and we are again looking into Dave's face. He is still seated on the backyard swing, recalling memories of the events that preceded and followed his wife's tragic accident]

Dave
Yes Father, I do remember the things I said and the prayer that I prayed in the woods a few weeks after Cecelia's death. . . .

[A misty, dreamlike fog settles in; then slowly fades and dissolves into another scene from the past to reveal yet another memory]

It's almost dark and Dave is kneeling in the woods, dressed in a camouflage bow-hunting outfit praying. Next to him on the ground is a hunting bow and arrows. He kneels there raising his hands skyward as he prays passionately.

Dave

[sobbing, tears running down his face, and praying loudly]
Dear God, I'm broken, I'm beaten, I'm at the bottom of the barrel, and I've got nothing left. If you're there, please take my life and use me! My heart is sick and my mind reels as I try to deal with not one but two of the most devastating events in my life at the same time: the tragic loss of my children's mother and the realization that I failed her miserably as a husband!

[Pauses; tears stream down his face, as he looks heavenward]

I've been living so selfishly, Lord; focusing on my career, my hobbies, my schedule, and the things that I enjoy. Please forgive me for doing that, and for thinking of church as a social club and a place to show off my musical talents. Right now, more than any other time in my life, I desperately need to know that you are real—and that you really are there!

[Pauses; then cries out with great passion and urgency]
Lord Jesus, if you're really there and you can hear me, please come into my heart and fill me with your holy spirit. I've lived for myself all these years, but now I just wanna live for you! I'm a broken, beaten man, but if I still have anything left, please take it and use it for your glory. Take my gifts, take my talents, take my life, and use them any way that you wish and any way that you can. Here I am, Lord; send me! I accept you, Jesus, as my Lord and savior, and I dedicate the rest of my life to serving you and others.

[Again, a misty, dreamlike fog rolls in; as this scene fogs, fades and dissolves into a close-up of Dave's face. He is still sitting on the backyard swing, nodding thoughtfully and with conviction]

[Abrupt cut to a new scene]

Dave is standing in the kitchen of their home, talking on a wall-mounted telephone. The scene changes to the office of the Christian school. Outside the principal's office in the main office, a sweet, kindly older woman with glasses answers the phone on her desk.

Ruth
Good morning, Lima Christian School.

Dave
Good morning, this is Dave Tripiciano; may I speak to Ron Davis? He's expecting my call.

Ruth
[Smiling and helpful]
Certainly, Mr. Tripiciano. Just a moment please. **[Pushes a button]** Ron can you take a call from Dave Tripiciano?

Ron Davis
[On phone in his office, smiling]
Yes, I've been looking forward to hearing from him.

Dave
[On the phone in his kitchen]
Good morning sir, this is Dave "Trip" getting back to you as promised; but I've got a funny feeling that you already know what my answer's gonna be.

Ron Davis
[smiling broadly]
Well, we've all been prayin' and hoping.

Dave
After some serious thought, and lots of prayer, I realize that I would have to be deaf, dumb, and blind not to see that God wants to use my gifts and experience at your school, so I have no other choice but to take the job.

Ron Davis
[smiling, very pleased]
That's great news Dave! You just made my day. Welcome aboard!

Dave
[Light chuckle]
I guess when God sets up a job interview for you, customizes the job to fit your schedule, and then offers your wife a job at the same place, you better take that job. Besides, I made a promise to him a few years ago in the woods that I have to keep.

Ron Davis
I was pretty sure you'd feel that way with so many things working together here for you, Mary, and the kids.

Dave
Much as I hate to go back into teaching, it'll be rewarding to give something to kids that might not get the chance to play in a good band otherwise, and it will be nice for Mary, the kids, and I to ride together every morning and be in the same building.

Ron Davis

Very good Dave, I'll see you guys at the teacher's meetings the day after Labor Day. Be here at eight o'clock for coffee. You can sign contracts and fill out some other paperwork that day.

Dave

Thanks a lot Ron; see you then.

Ron Davis

See you then, looking forward to working with you. Bye.

[The band room from the opening scene a few months later]

This time the room is filled with students, instruments and music:

Dave is right in the middle of a band rehearsal and the band is playing a piece of music. Smiling, he is waving his arms and pointing at different instruments as he conducts. There are approximately thirty students—a mixture of junior high and senior high—playing trumpets, trombones, saxophones, clarinets, flutes, tubas, and drums. Betsy is standing up in the back, playing a keyboard. The band is playing a marching band arrangement of "Shine Jesus Shine." Everyone seems to be playing with a lot of energy and enthusiasm, and as our gaze moves from one eager young face to the next it's clear that the students are really enjoying themselves.

Dave nods and yells encouragement to the kids as they play, smiling proudly and flashing the thumbs-up sign to one of the instrumental sections. The band sounds surprisingly good and quite powerful for a small group of student musicians. The song ends with a loud chord, and the students nod and smile with pride.

They are excited, and as a few begin to talk among themselves, Dave raises his hands to quiet them down so he can speak.

Dave

[In a loud voice]

All right, all right now, listen up! Listen up now. Wow! **[Pauses, looking at each student's face]** You guys have come a long way since the beginning of the year; you're really starting to sound great!

[As our gaze moves quickly down the rows of young faces, we see that the kids are sitting up attentively and seem to be very proud of the way they sound and the things their director is saying]

That was amazing! I can't believe a sound that big can come out of a band this small.

[A close-up of Betsy shows that she is nodding and also smiling proudly in agreement]

I'm very proud of you!

I've got some great news. The band director from Geneseo said we could have their old band uniforms, if we want 'em. They're dusty and pretty old, and they've been in a closet for a long time. But in their day they were expensive, beautiful uniforms and they just happen to be our school colors—blue and white! We're going to send them to the cleaners and then get some moms together to have a uniform sewing party to make them look new again, and maybe even add a few extra touches to make them our own!

[A buzz of conversation starts and the students are wide-eyed with excitement as they smile happily. Some eagerly turn to the person next to them to discuss the news. Betsy continues to smile and nod happily as she gives a thumbs up to one of her friends.]

Dave

[restoring order]

All right, all right now. I don't think I've ever worked with a bunch of kids who deserved to have their own band uniforms more than you guys do, but we better get back to work so when the uniforms get here we'll be sounding our best. Let's try "How Great Thou Art."

[The students rustle their papers as they fumble for the music. Then when it seems like everyone has found the piece and is looking his way, Dave raises his arms and starts the band.]

Once again, the band sounds very good on this marching band arrangement of the well-known hymn. The student's faces show great eagerness as they play. Dave smiles and nods with approval, giving a thumbs up to the drummers as they play a catchy beat; and then he makes eye contact with Betsy, who is proudly playing her part on the keyboard. Her admiration and respect for him is revealed in her eyes, as she follows his direction.

As the beloved hymn continues, the music swells to a powerful crescendo. The scene ends with a close-up of Dave who continues to smile broadly as he conducts enthusiastically with great passion.

[Fade to black]

Act 2 •
The High School Career Of A Band "Geek"

[Thirty years earlier] The dimly lit gymnasium of an older high-school building in a small town: (The year is 1965)

Dave is in a small gym that has been divided into two sections by a partition wall. We are on the "boys" side, seeing the scene through thirteen-year-old Dave's eyes. He is sitting on the gym floor, as a member of a boys' junior-high gym class. [The haircuts and dress of the boys and the gym teacher show that we're definitely in the "Leave It To Beaver" era]
The coach is holding a basketball while two boys, each with small groups of boys standing behind them, are choosing teammates from a rapidly diminishing group of other eager boys lined up along the sideline. They are choosing teams for a basketball game.

Team Captain #1
I'll take Tommy. C'mon, Tom.

[Tommy throws his arm up in a triumphant gesture as he bounds over to team number one with a big smile]

Team Captain #2
Skippy. I'll take Skippy Slayton.
[Skippy starts clapping loudly as he runs eagerly over to join team number two. Several teammates high-five him as he joins them]

The captains continue to pick teammates until there are only five not very athletic-looking boys left to be chosen, and Dave is one of them. Dave is physically the smallest of the group and has the slightest build.

Team Captain #1
Alex, c'mon man.
[Alex, feeling relieved to be chosen, quickly walks over to join his team.]

Team Captain #2
[Hesitating, he looks with disappointment at the boys still left]
Okay, Bobby. We'll take Bobby.

[Bobby, disappointed about being chosen so late in the game, reluctantly joins his group.]

[A few moments later] Only two boys are left. One of them is grossly overweight, to the point of being morbidly obese, and the other one is Dave. It's pretty clear they're embarrassed and self-conscious about being chosen last. They stare at the floor, nervously shuffling their feet.

Team Captain #1
[Hesitates]
Awright, awright, we'll take Tubby Tabone. You guys have got Trip.

Team Captain #2
[Whines]
Awww— man! We had Trip last time!

Gym Teacher
[Blows whistle; shouts]
Awright you guys, let's go! Play ball! **[He bounces the basketball to Captain #1]**

[Captain #1 bounces the ball to a teammate as he points out his starting five, and the opposing captain does the same. Boys begin to run back and forth, then up and down the gym, as loud yelling mingles with the sound of a basketball being dribbled.

Dave
[Dejectedly slides down the wall and slumps to the floor along the sideline with the other subs. The action around him becomes a noisy blur of motion. As the scene begins to fade, a close-up of his face shows sadness, hurt and embarrassment.]

[Fade to black]

[Dave is sixteen]

Dave's bedroom at his parent's house: a small, basic rectangular room in a newer house with a bed, night stand, dresser, and desk; a large, upright reel-to-reel tape recorder is turning on the desk. Dave is sitting in a chair, playing the trumpet and recording himself. His bedroom door (to his back) is closed and he's facing the music book propped up in his trumpet case which is resting on the bed. He is playing many fast scales and arpeggios and sounds quite impressive for someone his age.

[There's a knock on the closed door]

Dave's Father
[A tall, solidly built man, clearly of Italian descent (with dark hair and a large nose); opens the door and leans into the room, still holding the doorknob]

That sounds really good man, but it's time for supper. Better wash up and come quick before it gets cold. I hear a big improvement in your playing since you started taking lessons from Uncle Sy, but do you really have to practice three hours a day?

Dave

I'm not any good in sports and the other guys pick on me 'cause I'm small. When I fool around in class to try to look cool, the girls just laugh at me and tease me. Maybe if I become a famous trumpet player and professional musician, they'll see that I'm someone great—not just an oddball or a weirdo.

Dave's Father

Well, anything worth doing is worth doing well, and you seem to have the desire and the discipline to succeed. But you can't just hole up here, playing the trumpet all through high school. You remind me of a woodchuck hiding out in his hole. I wish you would hang out with the guys sometimes, or maybe even call a cute girl on the phone.

Dave

[softening and a little sad]

That would be great, if any of the guys or girls thought I was worth spending time with or getting to know better, but maybe when I'm a famous musician they'll all want to hang out with me. I'll show 'em, you'll see.

The kitchen of Dave's house, several hours later: Dave is in bed, and his mother and father are seated at the kitchen table talking. His dad sips a cold drink, and his mother is smoking a cigarette.

Dave's Mother
[A short, round-faced woman with short, dark hair and a round nose; also obviously of Italian descent]
I'm worried about your son. All he does is practice that trumpet. Saturday night I had to go out to the driveway in my pajamas. He was practicing the trumpet in the steamed-up car with the windows rolled up at one o'clock in the morning! Do you know what he said when I told him to come in? He said: "I didn't have the chance to get in three hours today, so I had to come out and finish in the car, but I wasn't bothering anybody."

Dave's Father
He's got talent and he's starting to sound good, but he sees becoming a great trumpet player as the way to escape from being the little nerdy kid, and to prove himself to the kids that pick on him and make fun of him.

Dave's Mother
I think it was a mistake to put him in kindergarten when he was only four. He's been the smallest and youngest kid in his class ever since.

Dave's Father
I wish he'd get a few good friends or a girl "friend" to hang out with. He's always hiding out in his room, like a woodchuck in his hole; but I do admire his passion to work hard at something that he really wants to do. Who knows, maybe he will be a famous trumpet player someday, or have a career in music. Three of my brothers made money playing in bands.

Dave's Mother
He wants to go to college for music. I hope he can find a job or make enough money to support a family with that kind of a degree.

Dave's Father
Well, I guess the best thing to do is encourage him, let him do something that he loves, and let nature take its course. He'll be all right.

[Abrupt cut to a new scene]

Back in the same high-school gym again, but it's two years later. Dave and many of the same boys from the basketball scene are now in senior high school. The boys stand on the sideline while the gym teacher shouts out names, taking roll call. The teacher is a heavy-set, arrogant man, puffed up with a sense of his own importance. He seems intent on showing the kids how tough and manly he is. He seems to be enjoying the fact that he has been placed in a position of authority over these boys, and likes to remind them that he's "the boss."

Coach Townsend
Tommy Price?

Tommy
[raises his hand]

Coach Townsend
[checks Tommy's name off the class list on the clipboard (he does the same thing after each boy's response)]

Coach Townsend
James Johnson?

James
[raises his hand]
Right here Coach.

Coach Townsend
Joey Davis?

Joey
[halfheartedly waves]
Here.

Coach Townsend
Jimmy Tabone?

Jimmy
[The obese boy from the basketball scene raises his hand halfway]
Present.

Coach Townsend
[Pauses, hesitates, then calls louder than on the previous names]
Pansy Dave Tripiciano

[There is an awkward silence; then some soft giggling, as a couple of the boys look at each other, smiling]

Dave
[In shock, his eyes widen fearfully as he stares at the floor, unable to respond]

Coach Townsend
[loudly] *Pansy* Dave Tripiciano, are you here?

Dave
[scared to death, whimpering]
H- h- here, Coach.

Coach Townsend
[with disdain and disgust]
I need to know if you're here, Mr. Tripiciano, because I need to know if you have to leave gym early again today, to go to *baaand praaactice!* **[He says the words "band practice" in a high-pitched, effeminate, whiney tone. Teasing and mocking Dave, as if to say that band practice isn't a manly pursuit]**

The gym erupts with laughter and giggling; as boys shake their heads and turn to smile at one another.

Dave
[As the laughter continues, the camera closes on Dave and the rest of the room becomes a blur. He stands with his shoulders slumped and his head down, staring at the floor. As the scene fades to black a close-up of his face shows deep sadness, hurt and embarrassment.

[Fade to black]

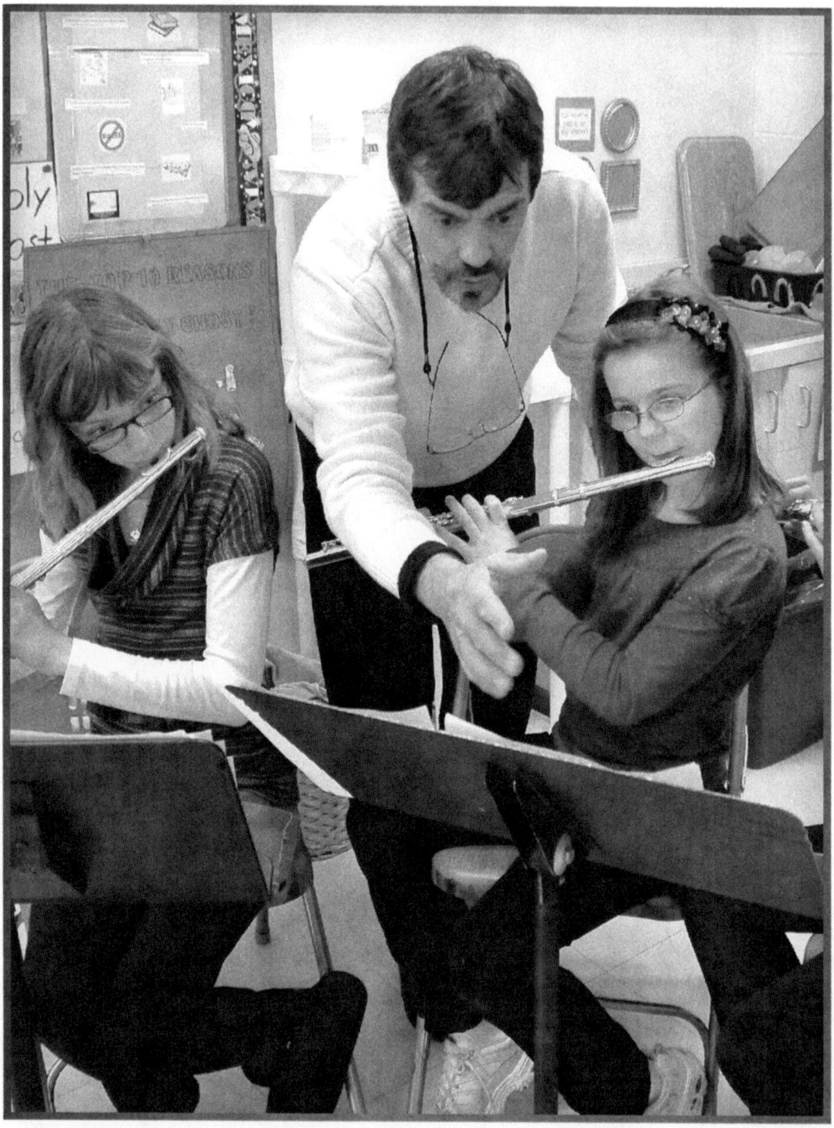

Act 3

Being A Hero In The Eyes Of A Child – Priceless

[Thirty years ahead in time, during Dave's first year teaching the band at the Christian school] In the same small band room.

Dave is giving a trumpet lesson to a small (slightly built) junior-high boy who looks a lot like Dave did at that same age. Dave is kneeling beside him as he plays, with his finger touching the page, pointing out each note for the boy. He is smiling, nodding with approval, and doing everything he can to encourage the youngster and make it clear that he loves him. [As the youngster finishes, Dave speaks.]

Dave
[enthusiastically]
Yes! That was awesome Matt; you're the man! **[Dave high-fives Matt and the boy nods proudly, smiling as Dave praises him.]** You've come a long way in a short time, and I'm proud of you. In fact, you've been working so hard I'm gonna give you a special honor. I know you're only a seventh-grader, but how would you like to march with the marching band in our very first parade on Memorial Day?

Matt
[smiling shyly]
That would be exciting, but I'm not sure I can march and play at the same time, and I wouldn't want to mess up the band.

Dave

[encouragingly]

No problem, there's nothing to it. I'll give you some really easy music to play and I'll train you. By the day of the parade, marching while you're playing will be as easy as breathing, and look at this! **[he quickly crosses the room to a uniform on a hanger, and Matt follows]** If you're in the marching band, you get to wear a blue and white uniform like this. Pretty cool, huh? These were old, dusty uniforms that we got for free, and they're even our school colors! We sent them to the cleaners and several of the band moms did some sewing. We added white sashes, new shoulder braids, and a chain across the hat brim. We even got new plumes, and I found some plastic crosses for the front of the hats. Here, check it out man. **[He picks up a band hat, complete with a tall white plume, and places it on the boy's head, smiling]**

Matt

[Turns to look in the mirror; beaming and nodding ecstatically in approval]

Wow! These are cool hats Mr. Trip. I can't wait to try on my uniform. I'll work hard and try to play my best.

Dave

[smiling proudly at the boy]

What a great combination! You look great — and your attitude's great. That's what makes a great band. I know you'll give your best effort, Matt; I know you will buddy. **[Dave lovingly places his hand on the boy's shoulder and pats it a couple of times. Looking off, over the boy's head, he nods happily, as if day-dreaming] The camera closes on his upper torso showing his arm and hand still going down to the boys shoulder. We see only Dave's head and shoulders, the top of the band hat and the plume as the scene starts to fog and blur, but instead of a fade out the foggy, dream like scene begins to clear and focus.**

As the scene clears and the camera starts to pull back, Dave still has his hand on the boy's shoulder, but the boy is now in full uniform. It's the day of the parade and they are outdoors, surrounded in a close huddle by the entire band with everyone in uniform. Dave has his other hand on Betsy's shoulder. All heads are bowed. As the large group of students presses in around their "coach," he is praying with and for his students before their first parade. It's a beautiful, sunny spring morning. [Dave prays]

Dave

Thank you Father, for giving me the opportunity to work with such a great group of kids, for using my gifts; and for allowing them to have this experience and this memory today. Thank you so much, for giving us these uniforms, and for the parents who made them look so great. Please let us sparkle and shine on this street today. Use our attitude, our marching, and the Christian music we play to touch hearts and lives for you. In Jesus' name we pray, amen.

[As he finishes the prayer, eyes open and heads come up. It's clear that the kids are very excited about being part of this parade, as many happy, eager young faces look toward Dave with love, admiration, and great respect. Dave pats Betsy and Matt's shoulders as he surveys the group (with a big smile). He is so proud and excited that he starts to tear up]

You guys look great, and we caught a beautiful day. I can't tell you how proud I am of all of you and how much it means to me to be part of this. I've had bands march for the Buffalo Bills and win a state championship, but right now none of that means as much as seeing you get to march in your first parade, and be a living, marching billboard for Christ. I know you're gonna look and sound

To View A Very Touching Live Video Of This Scene
Please Go To You Tube: http://youtu.be/Vjh7RTT9Va8

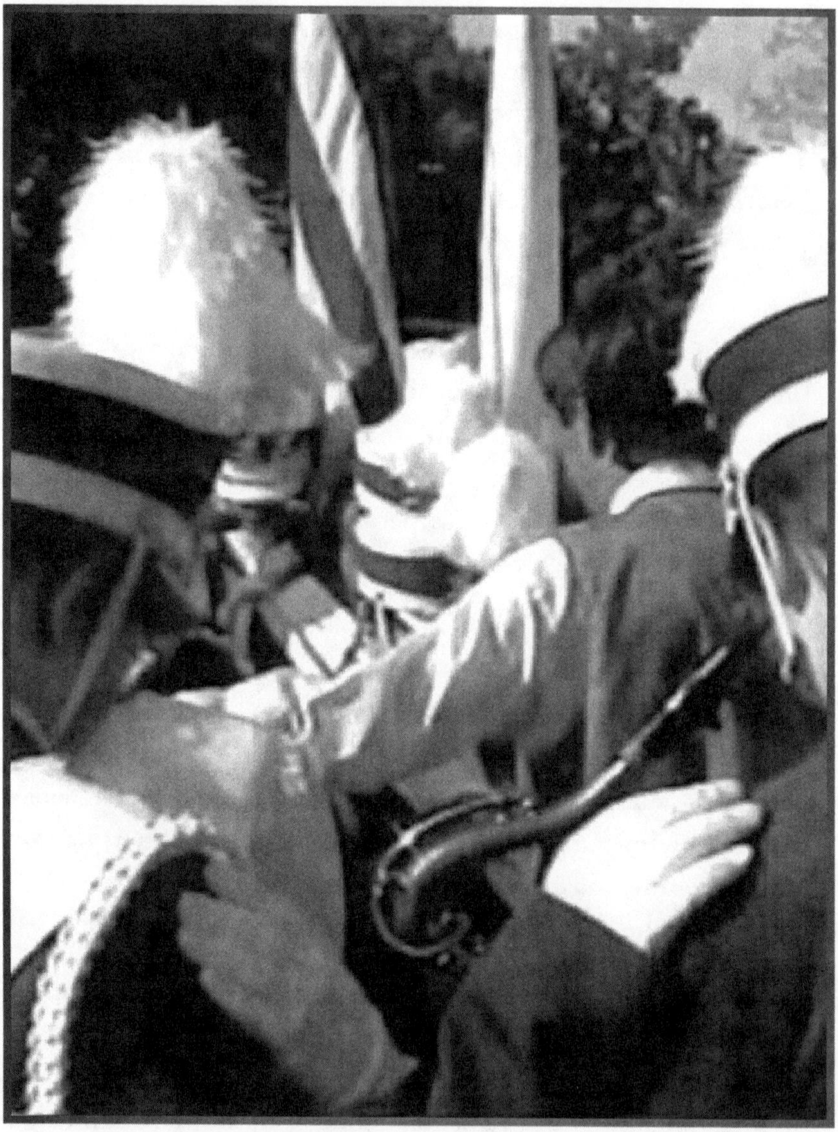

great! So carry yourself with pride and dignity, play with all your heart, and remember who you're marching for. **[shouts happily]** Let's go get'em now! Fall in!

[There is a blur of activity as the students slip on white gloves, ask Dave questions, strap on drums, and fall into line. They are excited and nervous. They smile, talk eagerly, and adjust each other's uniforms. Dave in the midst of three students, points to show them where to line up. There are the random sounds of horns tooting and drums pounding]

Betsy
[Loudly blows a whistle; shouting like a drill sergeant]
Sai——— nts! Ten hut!!

[The students stop whatever they're doing and snap to attention. Throughout the band, students proudly stand erect, with shoulders back and chin up. Some are smiling proudly while others have the look of a Marine Corps poster. Matt, holding his trumpet, is trying so hard to stand up straight that he is overdoing it and looks comical. Betsy stands proudly at the front of the band, facing her peers. She has an air of poise and confidence as she points, gives instructions, and takes charge of the group. She carries herself with great pride and dignity, and her eyes reveal the fact that this moment means a great deal to her]

[Abrupt cut to a new scene]

The entire band is coming down the street, playing loudly as they approach and the group completely fills the screen. They are playing a jazzy, marching-band arrangement of "When The Saints Go Marching In" and they look like they are going to march right out of the screen and into the theater. The bright

spring sun brings out the deep blue color of the uniforms and makes the white sashes and plumes sparkle in sharp contrast.

They sound and look very powerful and impressive for a small band and every student is standing tall and carrying their instrument in perfect playing position. As we see a few close-ups of students playing horns and drums, it's quite clear that everyone is giving their best effort and playing with all the heart and enthusiasm that they can. At the front of the band two young girls in matching outfits who seem to be a "matching pair" smile proudly as they carry a large blue banner that reads: Lima Christian School "Marching Saints" To God Be The Glory. In front of them a pretty blonde girl carries her flag and herself in a very dignified military posture. She is wearing a well-made but obviously homemade white majorette uniform with blue trim (and no hat). A slight breeze makes her white flag stand straight out, revealing a large royal-blue cross. By her side is a dark-haired girl wearing the same type of uniform and carrying herself equally well. Her flag is also white, but instead of a cross it has a large blue Christian fish emblem.

[The crowd, including many band parents, cheers, and applauds]

Parent Spectator #1
"Yea, Mr. Trip!"

Parent Spectator #2
"Go Lima Christian!"

Parent Spectator #3
"Way to go Betsy!"

[Other spectators not connected with the school show looks of surprise and admiration as they point, smile, applaud, and nod with approval. Meanwhile the band—musicians, flag bearers, Betsy, and Dave—continues to play and march impressively past us]

Toward the end of the band lineup, a stocky, older boy playing the snare drum concentrates intensely and with his eyes focused straight ahead he marches and plays earnestly. We see a close-up of his drumsticks rolling and tapping out the staccato rhythms that accompany the song, and the snare drum becomes louder than the rest of the band as the scene fades.

[Fade to black]

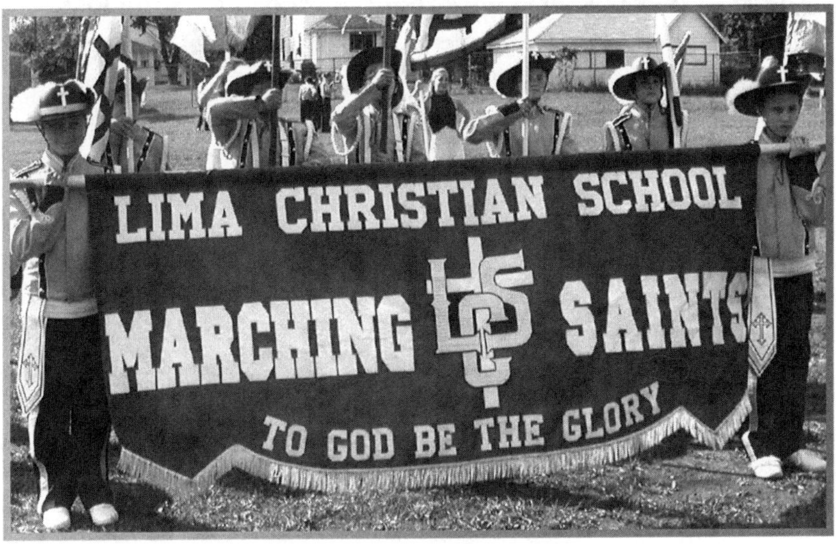

[Thirty minutes later] **A parking lot at the end of the parade:**

Dave is carrying a bass drum toward a long, white van lettered with the words "Lima Christian School." He is surrounded by a small group of his students who are now half in and half out of their uniforms and carrying instruments. The happy, excited students smile and talk eagerly as they share their memories from the parade. The group is walking through a parking lot filled with the rest of Dave's students and their parents; some of the students are changing out of their band uniforms at their parents' vehicles, putting instruments away, etc. Some of the parents are happily working together to load large band instruments into the school van.

The atmosphere is one of joy and accomplishment. Everyone smiles as they talk all at once about how great the band looked and sounded. Female students hug each other while male students exchange handshakes and high-fives.

Band Student #1
That was amazing!

Band Student #2
[gives Band Student #1 a high-five]
We were awesome!

Parent
[pats both of the students on the back]
You guys sounded great!

Dave
[ad lib actions and lines as he passes each student: high-fiveing some, hugging others, shaking hands with yet others, and patting some on the top of their band hats] You're the man! Great

job! Proud of you! We did it! What a sound! Great job drummers! Way to go! You're the woman! You guys were great! [etc.]

Band Student Mom
[Grabs her husband by the arm and turns him, then points in Dave's direction. Together they approach Dave near the middle of the parking lot. She begins to applaud loudly and deliberately. Her husband gets the idea and joins her as she honors Dave]

One by one parents all around the parking lot stop whatever they are doing, turn to face Dave and join the applause. The students, who were walking with him step back from him, face him, and also join the noisy ovation. Soon every person in the parking lot is standing, facing Dave, and enthusiastically applauding and cheering.

Dave
[Holding a bass drum while standing in the middle of the parking lot. He is deeply touched, and becomes overcome by emotion. He smiles, nodding with appreciation as tears well up in his eyes]

[Fade to black]

Act 4

Working Passionately To Prove Myself To Others

[The winter of 1969] In the basement boiler room of Dave's high school in Auburn, New York:

The concrete floor is dirty in this basement area which served as the boiler room at Dave's high school. There are two large boilers, a furnace, hot water tanks, duct work, exposed pipes, plumbing fittings, gauges, and valves.

The room is noisy with the sounds of the furnace and other machinery running. Over all the noise, we faintly hear the sound of a trumpet playing intricate scales and exercises. As the scene moves through the room and around to the backside of the boilers, the sound of the trumpet grows louder and louder. In a dusty, cobweb-filled corner behind the boilers there is a rusty folding chair illuminated by a single light bulb. Dave sits in the chair, playing his trumpet. He has a thick, heavy music book propped up on a lightweight, slightly bent folding music stand. He is practicing diligently and sounds more like an advanced conservatory student than a high-school boy.

As he plays, a school custodian enters the boiler room through the door behind him. The dark-haired older man is pushing a cleaning cart loaded with mops, brooms, a vacuum cleaner, and other cleaning supplies. The man stops short with a look of shock and surprise when he hears the trumpet and sees Dave there. Leaving his cart by the door he walks up behind Dave with an astonished look to question him.

Mr. DeMarco
What in the world are you doing here, son?

Dave
[startled, guilty; jumps up and turns]
Oh, Mr. DeMarco, I'm just practicing my trumpet. I didn't think I'd be bothering anybody, and with all this noise I was hoping nobody would even know I was down here.

Mr. DeMarco
[firmly]
This is a restricted area! Students aren't allowed in here! Do you have any idea what could happen if kids started coming in here, horsing around near all this machinery?

Dave
[pleading his case]
I'm not horsing around. I'm trying to get into a music college and win a scholarship, and I've got some auditions coming up. [**begging**] Please don't turn me in, Mr. DeMarco. I've got to get in three hours a day to have a chance, and my study hall teacher thinks I'm in the library. If you tell on me, I'll get in a lot of trouble and I won't be able to practice in school anymore.

Mr. DeMarco
[shaking his head but softening]
You're a Tripiciano, aren't ya? [**Dave nods**] If I recall, your grandfather and a couple of your uncles were musicians, weren't they? [**Dave nods again**] As a matter of fact, I remember taking the wife to dances in the old days up at the lake pavilion and hearing your Uncle Cooney play the trumpet in the Army Band.

[Pauses, looks down at the floor and then back at the scared, wide-eyed boy]

Well, if you were up to no good in here, you can bet your life you'd be in a heap of trouble. But it looks like you're trying to do something worthwhile and you're sure workin' pretty hard at it, so who am I to stomp on somebody's dream? **[smiling]** Besides, I admire ya kid, and ya sound good.

Dave
[relieved, thrilled, and thankful]
I can't thank you enough, sir. Thank you, very much!

Mr. DeMarco
[turns back toward his cart and smiling broadly he makes a joke as he exits]
I guess I'll just have to be like that big fat German prison guard on "Hogan's Heroes" **[Mimics a strong German accent, with a high-pitched voice]** *I s-s-see n-n-othing! I k-k-now n-n-othing!* **[then laughs]** Ha, Ha, Ha.

[Abrupt cut to a new scene]

[A few months later, June of 1969] Dave's high-school graduation:

Every seat of the large, high-school auditorium is filled with the parents and siblings of the graduates, most of them dressed in their Sunday best. There are very large, ornate windows along the left side wall, and the floor slopes downward dramatically from the doors in the back to the stage in the front. Heavy, theatrical curtains made of maroon velvet frame the stage and the words "West High School" are emblazoned on the wall above them.

The first ten rows in the center section are filled with the young men and women who are graduating, all uniformly dressed in

maroon caps and gowns. The other seats are filled with supportive friends, family, and teachers. Many of the parents are sporting the most popular snapshot cameras and home movie cameras. The sound of a trumpet and a piano fill the room, and the eyes of every person are fixed on one graduate standing center stage, playing the trumpet. A close up of the lone musician shows that it is Dave, standing proudly erect and aiming his trumpet confidently at the back doors as he performs a trumpet solo with tremendous passion and energy. An older, male faculty member, who is obviously an accomplished pianist, is accompanying him.

Dave is playing an extremely complex, sophisticated piece of music that one might expect to hear in a concert hall. He is performing flawlessly, with amazing virtuosity and sounds more like a professional musician than a high-school student. The audience shares in this sentiment, as they reveal looks of surprise, awe, and amazement. All those in attendance sit wide-eyed, nodding, smiling, or shaking their heads. Basketball Captain #1 is one of the graduates shocked and amazed by what he is hearing. Dave's father smiles proudly, and tears run down his mother's face. As Dave continues to play, we see Mr. DeMarco the custodian, standing backstage near the light panel. He is leaning on a push broom, smiling broadly and nodding as he watches through the curtains.

The music swells to a crescendo as Dave cascades effortlessly up and down arpeggios and skips flawlessly through dozens of very fast notes. Then the piece ends with a triumphant high note on the trumpet and a loud chord on the piano. While the sound of the final chord is still ringing through the room, loud cheers and shouts rise up from the audience, and they jump to their feet applauding enthusiastically. Everyone in the room is standing, including all of Dave's classmates. Dave, overcome

by emotion, bows his head and shoulders a couple of times to thank the audience; but the applause continues without subsiding. There is cheering, whistling, and applauding as the audience smiles and nods with approval or shakes their heads in amazement. Dave's father smiles proudly as he applauds, and Dave's mother simply stands with both hands firmly grasping the seat back in front of her, as tears run down her face. Mr. DeMarco [backstage] applauds eagerly, with a big smile as he quietly repeats the words:

Mr. DeMarco
Way to go kid, way to go!

[Several minutes later] The graduation ceremony conclusion:

The recessional music is playing as graduates, in two widely spaced single-file lines, slowly make their way up the two main aisles toward the back auditorium doors. Camera flashes are everywhere as family members snap pictures of their favorite graduate, and almost everyone in a cap and gown is wearing a happy smile. Dave stands tall, with his head held high, as he walks proudly up the aisle carrying his trumpet under his right arm. He exudes confidence, great accomplishment, and relief; his whole self-image has changed. [He thinks]

Dave
[in thought]
Yes! I did it! I showed 'em. I showed 'em that I'm not just an oddball or a nerd. I think I finally won their respect today!

[Outdoors, several minutes later]

Outside the front entrance of the high school it's a beautiful June day. Everyone is taking photos of the graduates (solo and with groups of friends or family); the graduates exchange hugs, high-fives, and handshakes. A few of the grads throw their hats in the air, and many of them now have their gowns unbuttoned or their hats or gowns off altogether. Many of the graduates receive congratulations from parents and family members, but quite a number of parents, faculty members, and classmates approach Dave to congratulate him and compliment his playing:

Male Parent

Great trumpet playing, young man! I never thought I'd ever hear someone your age play like that!

Dave

[humbly]

Thank you sir, thank you very much.

Female Parent

I never thought I'd hear anything like that outside of a concert hall. Are you going to major in music?

Dave

[graciously]

Thank you. Yes, I've been accepted at Fredonia State.

Two Female Grads [one speaks]

Wow, Trip, that was amazing! None of us girls realized you played like that. We couldn't believe it! You sounded like some professional musician that you'd hear on the Ed Sullivan show.

Dave

[smiling]

Well, I'm not ready for Ed Sullivan yet, but it means a lot to know that you guys think I am.

Two Male Grads

[one of them shakes Dave's hand, the other speaks]

Hey Trip, that was pretty unbelievable man. You know what the guys are saying? Some of the guys are sayin' things like: "I thought that kid was a nerd, but—man, he can sure play a horn!"

Dave

[delighted]

Thanks John, thanks a lot. That means a lot to hear that.

[Background music starts] Smiling adults and students continue to eagerly shake Dave's hand. He smiles graciously in return; then his mom and dad spot him and come over to congratulate him. His mom hugs him tightly for a long time as his dad, smiling, musses his hair and pats him on the shoulder.

[Fade to black]

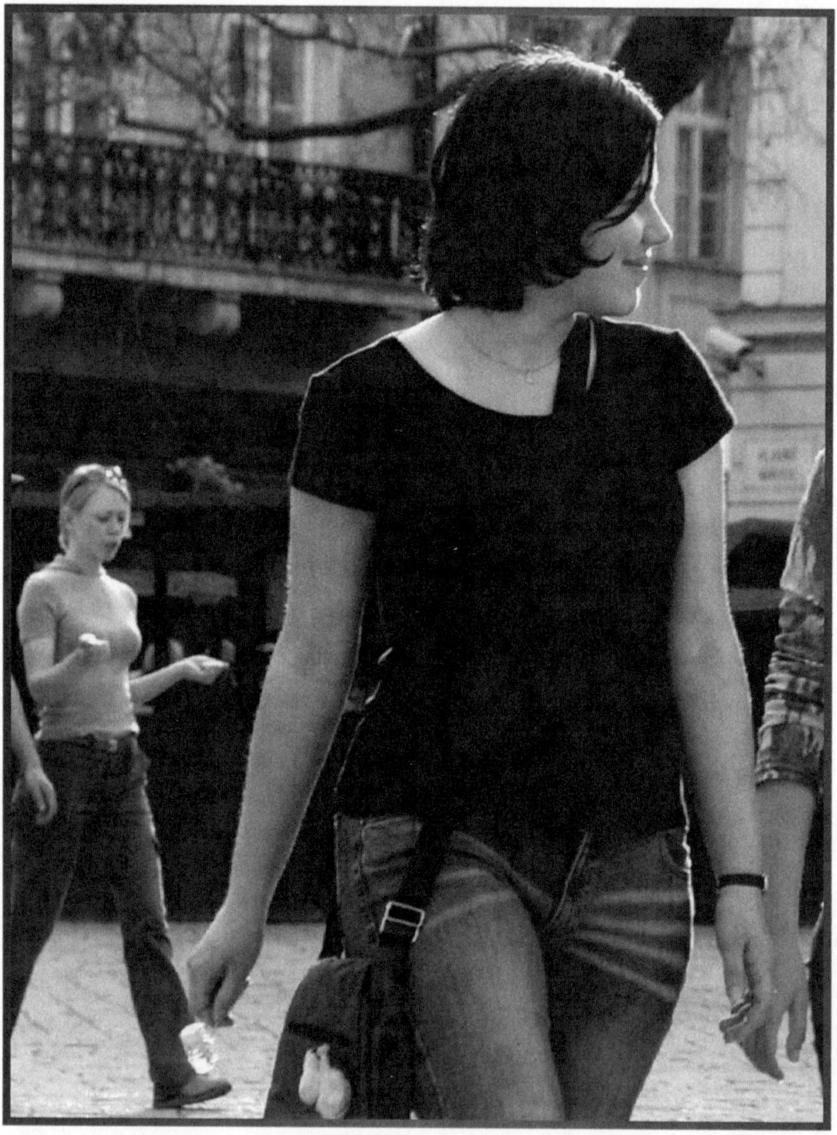

Act 5 •

A Kid Getting "Candy" For The First Time

[The fall of 1969] Dave is riding in a car with his mom and dad:

They are taking him off to college, and the car is filled with suitcases, boxes, a trunk, clothing, books, etc. Dave, now almost eighteen, has grown up quite a bit both in physical stature and self-confidence. College-age Dave is quite handsome, with thick dark hair, high cheek bones and large soft eyes. He has become the kind of young man that many girls would be attracted to. [He is riding in the back seat and his parents are in the front] As the car turns into a driveway between tall brick buildings, a large sign shows that they are entering the campus of the State University of New York College at Fredonia. As their car passes two attractive female students walking on the campus, his mother turns to him with a word of advice:

Dave's Mother
Watch out for these college girls; I've heard they can be quite flirty and very "loosey - goosey" these days. These are the '60s, and a lot of the college kids today believe in free love.

Dave
Never had many girls interested in me before, why would I now?

Dave's Mother

You don't realize it, but you've grown up to be quite a good-looking young man, and these girls have no idea what the girls you grew up with thought of you. To them, you're not the little nerdy kid that people made fun of; you're just that good-looking new guy with dark hair that plays the trumpet.

Dave

[doubtful]

Thanks for the vote of confidence and for trying to encourage me, mom, but I'll believe that kind of stuff when I see it.

Dave's Father

Just be careful man. Sometimes, if a young guy goes from no girlfriends, to all of a sudden lots of girls flirting and showing an interest. It can be like a kid getting candy for the first time. It becomes an addiction and you just can't get enough.

Dave

Thanks for the warnings guys, but I find it pretty hard to believe that really cute college girls like the ones we just passed would be interested in me.

[Abrupt cut to a new scene]

A week later at the college "welcome back" picnic:

At a state park near the campus, a large banner reads: "Welcome Back SUNY Fredonia Students," and several picnic tables are set up with food and drinks. Food service people in white uniforms and chef's hats are cooking and serving the students. There's a lake in the background and a large wooded area to the right side of the picnic area. College-age young adults are everywhere, grabbing food from picnic tables, eating, talking, laughing, and playing Frisbee, pouring and sipping cold drinks, and,

in general, having a great time. A small group of students are seated cross-legged in a circle on the grass. Some of them play guitars and sing while others without guitars just sing. They are dressed as "flower children" or "hippies" (a common look of the '60s). Some of the other students dressed more conservatively sit back away from the circle, almost as an "audience," listening, nodding, smiling, and/or singing along as they eat or sip drinks. Since this is an era where college students were allowed to smoke on campus and even inside college dining halls, several of the students are smoking cigarettes.

Dave, being a newcomer and a freshman, seems shy and self-conscious. He stands with a group of other young men who appear to be equally self-conscious. He has a hotdog in one hand and a drink in the other as he smiles and tries to strike up a conversation and a friendship with two portly freshmen boys.

Dave
[reaching out to shake hands]
You guys look like you're newcomers, like me. I'm Dave Trip from Auburn, New York. I'm a music major. Where ya from?

[The two chubby young men are quite pleased that a stranger has spoken to them, and they smile and respond eagerly to Dave's question]

Ted
[shakes hands with Dave, smiling]
Hi, Ted, Ted Bond, Grand Island, New York: **[in the tone of a tour guide]** "the biggest inland island in the world." I'm only here 'cause my parents made me come **[pauses]** liberal arts.

Robbie
[shakes hands; in a heavy New York accent]

Robbie Cesari, Central Islip, Long Island: **[smiling, he mimics Ted's tour-guide tone]** "The largest island in the United States (before they added Alaska and Hawaii)" **[pauses]** biology.

Dave

Whoa, nice accent man! You talk cool. The girls at my high school always went nuts over a guy that had any kind of an accent.

Robbie

I don't have an accent, you guys do. I could tell you guys were from upstate New York before you even said it, 'cause everybody talks funny up here. But, speaking of girls goin' nuts — that one over there **[points]** has been smiling and looking over here for the last ten minutes. I think she's trying to catch your eye Dave, because Ted and I aren't really the kind of guys that girls notice, let alone stare at.

Dave

[Surprised, looks quickly across to a picnic table where a group of four girls are seated. They are talking and giggling as they admire the "hippie" guitar players and point out good-looking young men to each other. A tall girl with short dark hair on the far side of the table is staring right at Dave. As he looks her way their eyes meet and a surprised smile comes to his face as well as hers. The girl elbows her friends and they all look his way then begin to talk and laugh excitedly among themselves. Dave's very pleased and excited, and his expression is one of great surprise, since he is not used to being the type of guy that girls look at or make a fuss over]

Ted

There you go man; here's your chance to meet a "college" girl. Don't blow it. Actually, this is a chance for all three of us to meet some girls. Please let us go over there with ya; a couple of them are kinda cute.

Dave

[Scared to death; looks nervously at the two other boys, then back across at the smiling group of girls who are now all looking in his direction. Squaring his shoulders and taking a deep breath, he strides boldly in their direction, with the other two boys eagerly following behind him. He walks right up to the girl with the short dark hair and greets her with a smile]

[turning on the charm] Hi, I'm Dave; we're new this year and we're trying to make some friends. Are you guys freshman?

Peg

[smiling flirtatiously]

The three of us are, but Ronnie there's a "big-time" sophomore. I'm Peg, from Binghamton; that's Sarah from Buffalo; Cindy from New Jersey; and Ronnie from Long Island.

Robbie

[eagerly]

I'm from the island too! South shore or north shore?

Ronnie

[heavy New York accent]

South shore, near Fire Island. My dad owns a marina there.

Robbie
[ecstatic]
Oh, thank you, thank you! Finally somebody who talks normal! These guys are trying to tell me that I have an accent, can you imagine that! They're the ones with the accent, not me.

Ronnie
[laughing and going along]
They are the ones with the accent; we're the ones who talk normal.

Dave
So what are you guys majoring in? I'm a music major.

Peg
Cindy and I aren't really sure what we want to do yet, so we're both liberal arts majors.

Sarah
I'm a social studies major; I wanna go into politics.

Ronnie
I love kids and I've wanted to be a teacher my whole life, so I'm in elementary education; hope I can get a job though.

Dave
This is Ted, he's in liberal arts too; and that's Robbie, he's a biology major. You guys staying for the bonfire? You're welcome to hang out with us and sit with us at the fire, if you are.

Peg
[thinking fast]
Well, Ronnie has a car and she was just getting ready to take all of us back to the campus. But I really would rather stay for the bonfire, if I had someone to sit with. I wouldn't mind staying and hanging out with you, Dave. Does your offer stand for just you and me?

Dave
[Looks eagerly at Ted and then at Robbie to get their approval. The two other boys, though disappointed, are not surprised by her response; and even though they're not included, they want to at least see Dave have the opportunity for his first date with a college girl]

Robbie
[forcing a smile]
Actually, I just remembered that I've still got a lot of unpacking to do before classes start, so I really should be getting back to the campus. You guys have a good time.

Ted
I'm pretty tired, and if the wind is blowin' the wrong way the smoke from a fire makes me sneeze. You guys enjoy it for me. Don't do anything I wouldn't do. C'mon, Robbie, I'll walk you back.

The girls say their goodbyes to Peg and the three boys, with all the standard lines ["nice meeting you," "take care," "have a good year," "call us tomorrow Peg," etc.] As the girls talk for a moment in a group, Dave shakes hands with Robbie and Ted.

He says goodbye and thanks them. Robbie gives him a knowing smile and nods his approval. Ted gives him a sly wink and a thumbs up.

[Hours later, after dark] At a large bonfire at the same park:

A wide circle of young people several rows deep hang out around a large, crackling bonfire. The fire sends flames and sparks quite high into the air. The group of "flower children" guitarists and singers are seated on one side of the fire, still leading those who wish to sing along in their protest songs of the '60s.

Dave and Peg are seated in the front row of the circle on the opposite side of the fire. They sit close together, leaning into one another as the mellow flickering light from the fire illuminates their faces. They are smiling and talking easily. Dave leans into Peg's ear as he says something, elbowing her playfully at the same time. She smiles and nods in agreement, touching his arm as they both laugh. It's clear that their friendship has deepened quickly and they are enjoying each other's company.

Dave
[smiling]
Wow, it sounds like your little brother is quite a character.

Peg
Oh he is—he sure is; he drives me crazy!

The male "hippie" guitar player (with long dark hair and a mustache) and the girl "flower child" (with long, straight blonde hair and a braided flower headband) sit cross-legged on the grass strumming and singing loudly. Another girl "flower child" closes her eyes as she opens her hands and raises them skyward, her arms bent at the elbows as she sways back and

forth humming and singing with the music, almost as if she is in a trance. . . .

Peg (smiling) also sways slightly to the music. She looks at Dave's face for a moment then back into the fire as she reaches for and then grasps Dave's hand. Dave's eyes widen with surprise as Peg leans into him and rests her head on his shoulder. Dave, delighted but clearly inexperienced, awkwardly puts his arm around her, and a knowing smile spreads across Peg's face.

Peg
[happy and content]
It's getting pretty warm here by the fire, wannna go for a walk?

Dave
[smiling, thrilled]
Yeah, that would be great, let's go.

[He stands, then reaches down for Peg's hand and pulls her to her feet]

They walk hand in hand through the park, alone in the moonlight. There's a crescent moon hanging in the sky overhead as they approach the entrance to one of the hiking trails that leads into the woods.

Peg
What a beautiful night! I love moonlit nights and the smell of fall.

Dave [smiling, teasing]
Shall we take this trail and see where it leads? You're not one of those wimpy girls that are afraid to walk through the woods in the dark, are ya?

Peg
[also joking, teasing]
I don't know, I guess it depends on who I'm with and how safe I feel. **[Changing her tone to that of a wide-eyed, innocent, young girl, she tries to imitate Dorothy from "*The Wizard Of Oz*" as she asks Dave a question using a paraphrased line from the movie]**
"Do you think there are any horrible monsters or man-eating beasts in these woods, Tin Man?"

Dave
[Without missing a beat, he adopts and mimics the voice and attitude of the Tin Man and responds with a line from the movie]
"Some, but mostly lions and tigers and bears."

Peg
[grasps Dave's hand tightly and crouches slightly (pretending to be scared), then starts forward into the woods, looking back and forth with wide eyes as she repeats:]
Lions and tigers and bears, oh my! Lions and tigers and bears, oh my! Lions and tigers and bears, oh my!

[A few moments later: The couple is farther down the trail, well into the woods. Peg is laughing and swinging Dave's hand happily as she chants the same line slowly and softly (almost in a whisper) under her breath a few more times] Lions and tigers and bears, oh my! Lions and tigers and bears, oh my!

[She stops walking and turns to Dave, still holding his hand. Looking into his face, she reaches up slowly with her free hand to the back of his head. Pushing her open fingers through his hair, she leans into him; pulling his face to hers, she opens her mouth slightly and begins to kiss him. Dave, surprised and a little awkward at first, quickly gets the idea. His arms surround her and his hands caress her back and shoulders as he moves his head slowly back and forth. As the long kiss continues, Peg let's go of his hand and brings her hand up and around the back of his shoulder. They continue to kiss passionately]

[Fade to black]

[Three days later] A band rehearsal in the college music building: A college concert band is rehearsing in a large, well-equipped band room in the building that houses the college music department. There are tubas hanging on the back wall and bass fiddles on a rack along the right side wall. The room has steps or tiers for each row of instruments in a semicircular formation that descend to a central point, where the conductor is seated on a tall pivoting stool with a high back. His stool rests on an elevated platform, and as he energetically conducts the group he is visible from anywhere in the room. The band is playing a complex piece of music at full volume. Dave is the first in a row of nine trumpet players, playing confidently in the very back row. Young men and women are playing clarinets, flutes, saxophones, a tuba, and percussion instruments with much pride and expertise as they follow the conductor's guidance.

Suddenly, the conductor waves his hands and stops the group in the middle of the piece. It takes a few seconds before everyone realizes that he has stopped and stops playing.

Conductor

Very nice, very nice; ladies and gentlemen, thank you. Alto saxophones, I would like you to play at number forty-seven for me please. I need your articulation to be very exact there. Please be careful to notice which notes are slurred and which ones are tongued, and make your tonguing more staccato. One, two, and . . .

[As the alto saxophones play a section for the conductor and the rest of the group sits idle, the trumpet player next to Dave, turns toward him and elbows him]

Andy

[quietly]

Holy cow! That redheaded flute player in the front row has the prettiest face I've ever seen that wasn't in a movie or on TV. I can't stop looking at her! She keeps looking back here too, and it's driving me crazy!

Dave

Wow! You're right; she does have a beautiful face. She looks like a princess from a Disney movie or a Barbie Doll. She must have a couple dozen boyfriends, though.

[Just as he is looking at the girl and saying that, the pretty young redhead turns to look right at him. When she sees that Dave is staring at her, she gives him a very nice smile and then turns back to face the front. Dave and the boy next to him look wild-eyed at each other]

Conductor

Okay people, you've been working pretty hard this morning so I'm going to give you a ten-minute break. Then we'll come back and play straight through the Holst Suite — from beginning to end.

[Everyone shuffles around, most of them out to the hallway just outside the band room, where they mill about and socialize during the break. The sound of a few random instruments comes from inside the fairly empty band room. A few students hold their instruments in the hallway, and others hold or sip soft drinks from the soda machine nearby.

The pretty red-haired flutist is leaning with her back against the wall near the band room door, holding her flute. Dave and his "partner in crime," Andy, have her "surrounded" and are trying to make an impression on her. Sidekick Andy has one hand on the wall next to her and is leaning somewhat aggressively toward her as he speaks, but she is smiling graciously at the two of them and doesn't seem to mind this. Dave, more shy, polite, and unsure of himself, is hanging back, keeping a little more distance, but he smiles sincerely, taking a genuine interest in her as they talk.

Andy

Where are you from, and what high school did you go to?

Lynn

I'm from Jefferson, a small town in Ohio. We only had one high school in our town and the band program wasn't all that great. I'm probably the first person to go off to college to major in music from our high school in ten years or more.

Dave
[awkwardly blurting out]
You're a very pretty girl; I bet you have lots of boyfriends!

Lynn
[blushing, but very flattered]
Actually, I come from a very old-fashioned Mennonite family. We're not allowed to date anyone until we're eighteen. That'll be next month for me, but I can't believe how many nice boys I've met here already.

Andy
[looking into the band room]
Uh Oh! Looks like Dr. Greenwood wants us back in there.

[Students slowly file past the threesome and back into the band room, as they wrap up their conversation]

Dave
Very nice meeting you, Lynn; maybe I'll see you around the building and we'll be able to talk more another time.

Lynn [smiling, sincerely]
Hope so, it was nice meeting you guys.

Andy
Good talking to you Lynn, catch you later.

[Back in the band room during the rehearsal. The band is playing a soft woodwind section where the trumpets don't play, so Andy leans over and speaks to Dave quietly]

Andy
I can understand why she's already met so many "nice" boys here. With her looks, I wouldn't be surprised if every guy on this campus who's seen her has tried to hit on her.

Dave
Looking toward Lynn playing her flute in the front row:
[we hear his thoughts]
So beautiful, and yet so innocent and open, with almost no experience with guys: What an appealing combination! I think I'm in love. I hope I get the chance to talk to her again soon.

A small upstairs practice room in the music building the next day:

Dave is practicing his trumpet in a small, upstairs practice room in the music building. The window, the paint, and the woodwork in the room suggest a building that has been there for quite some time. He is standing up, with a music stand in front of him, while playing toward the open window. Against one wall is an old upright piano with his trumpet case on it. The only other furniture in the room is the beat-up chair behind him.

Through the open window, he looks out across an open courtyard into the windows of other similar rooms in the same building where other students are also practicing. As Dave plays rapid scales and arpeggios the sound of his trumpet mingles with the random sounds of a wide variety of other instruments coming through the open window and from the hallway outside the closed practice room door.

As he finishes a series of difficult exercises he brings his arms down, and still holding his trumpet, breathes a deep sigh. Moving to the window, he holds his trumpet in one hand as he

leans both elbows on the window sill and peers out the window. Yawning indifferently, he is taking a break and daydreaming as he looks into the different practice rooms across the way. As his eyes move from one lighted window to the next—he sees a female cellist practicing in one room and a male pianist in the next; Then he sees two French hornists playing a horn duet in the room next door to a female vocalist singing a powerful operatic aria; and as his gaze moves to the next room, his head stops abruptly and jerks back. No longer daydreaming, he is suddenly alert and very focused. The attractive female flutist in the next room has long, full, shiny red hair flowing down over her back and shoulders. Dave's eyes widen and his jaw drops, as he realizes that to his surprise and delight it's Lynn. Upon seeing her there he quickly crosses to the door and exits the room, still carrying his trumpet.

Walking quickly down the hall through a cacophony of instrument sounds, he heads for the hallway across the courtyard and toward the room where he saw Lynn. When he reaches the door to her practice room and sees her through the small window, he hesitates, chickens out, and turns to walk away. But after three or four steps he turns, squares his shoulders, strides boldly up to the door, and knocks politely.

Lynn
[opening the door and smiling, eagerly]
Dave! Good to see you. How ya doin? C'mon in.

Dave [entering the room]
Hey Lynn, how's it goin'? I was up here practicing, and I went for a walk to rest my lip and see who else was around tonight. When I heard the sound of a flute, I looked in and there you were.

Lynn
[joking]
Yep, here I am, living the lonely life of a music major. Practicing hours and hours each day in a tiny little room all by myself, far from friends and family, wondering if I'll ever be a great flutist or a music teacher, if I'll ever graduate from here, and if, someday, I'll actually have a career in music.

Dave
[chuckles]
Don't be so glum! Your playing sounds amazing to me, plus you've got the looks that will probably get you hired on the spot at any job you ever apply for. If you were a music teacher at my school, I would have had the biggest crush in the world on you!

Lynn
[She is flattered and blushes deeply as she smiles and thanks him; then smiling warmly]
Thanks, thanks a lot for saying that. I really needed a word of encouragement right now and it's nice having somebody to talk to. This is the first time I've been away from home for any length of time, and it does get lonely up here in these little rooms.

Dave
[moves to the chair and sits, motioning for her to come over]
C'mon, C'mon. I'll prove it to you right now that you're gonna be a great music teacher. I've never tried to blow a flute and I don't think I can make a sound on one. Teach me how to get a sound on a flute. Pretend that I'm one of your students.

Lynn

[Donning a "teacher" voice and a big smile, she takes the piece off her flute that you blow into and kneels next to Dave's chair] Okay now, "David", let's see if you can make a sound by blowing across the hole in the flute's head joint. Pucker your lips up into a pout and then blow a thin stream of air across the hole, like this.

[She demonstrates by puckering her lips into a pout just a couple of feet from Dave's face. She does this innocently, trying to teach him. But Dave is mesmerized by the closeness of her mouth and cannot take his eyes off of her lips. She then puts the silver tube to her mouth and blows across it, producing a high-pitched whistle! With that, she hands the mouthpiece to Dave]

Here, now you try it. Blow a very thin stream of air.

[Dave tries several times but can't seem to get it, making nothing more than funny-sounding huffing and puffing noises]

Lynn

That's okay, try it again, but shape your mouth like mine.

[This time she moves even closer, and in a sincere attempt to show him the lip position, she provocatively pouts and puckers her mouth just a few inches from his face. Again, Dave's eyes widen as he stares at her full lips, until finally, overcome with desire he moves in to kiss her softly but deeply on the mouth. Surprised, she tenses and almost pulls away, but then surrenders to his kiss, opening her mouth slightly and kissing him passionately in return. Their arms move to embrace each other during the long kiss]

[Fade to black]

The downstairs hallway outside the band room the next day:

As students move up and down the crowded hallway, Andy is taking his trumpet case out of a storage locker not far from the spot where he and Dave were talking to Lynn. Dave rushes up to him with a big smile, and grabs and shakes his arm with both hands. He is very excited and eager to tell him the big news.

Dave
[happily, excited]
I kissed the redheaded flute princess!!

Andy
[surprised and with disbelief]
No way! No way in the world!

Dave
Yes way! I certainly did! Last night in a practice room!

Andy
You dog! You sly dog you! Did she kiss you back?

Dave
[proudly]
She sure did, as a matter of fact we're kind of going together.

Andy
Holy cow! Incredible, unbelievable, what about Peg?

Dave

She was just some flirty, boy-crazy freshman girl trying to meet guys at the "welcome back" picnic. I don't think it really meant anything to her. She was probably bragging to all of her friends the next day that some guy took her for a walk through the woods in the moonlight and kissed her. That's what those types of girls like to do. Besides, Lynn is ten times prettier, much nicer, and a lot more innocent, too.

Andy

Wow, my buddy Dave the Rave is the "Casanova" of the music department! Can I have your autograph? Better yet, can I just follow you around and have the girls you decide you don't want? I'd be happy just to have your leftovers.

Dave

[offended]

That's mean. I'm not just some playboy; I really like Lynn, a lot. In fact, I might even be in love with her.

[Two days later] A campus walkway on a beautiful fall afternoon:

A few students with books and instrument cases walk along a sidewalk that runs through the center of the campus. The tree-lined walkway passes among stately brick and stone buildings, both modern and traditional. Dave is holding Lynn's hand as they walk together toward the music building in the distance. They both smile as they talk and laugh together and it's clear that they're developing a boyfriend-girlfriend relationship. Dave is so focused on Lynn that he does not notice Peg walking toward them with a group of her friends from the opposite direction. When Peg spots Dave holding hands with the pretty redhead, she wells up with anger, hatred, and jealousy. She walks quickly toward the happy couple, muttering all kinds

of things under her breath; but Dave never sees her coming—until it's too late.

Peg

[muttering in a rage as she walks]

So that's why you never tried to call me or return my calls after the picnic! You two-timing phony! Mr. **[whines]** "I never had many girls interested in me in high school." What a lie! What a liar! **[Shouts]** You're just a big jerk!

Dave

[surprised, as Peg approaches angrily]

Peg!

Peg

[yelling] Skirt chaser!! **[she kicks him quite hard]**

Dave

Oowhhh!!

[He falls to the ground, groaning in pain and clutching his leg. Lynn kneels to help and comfort him, but she is shocked and confused as she watches Peg and her girlfriends look back with nasty glances. As the girls walk away they continue to make crude remarks and gestures]

Dave

[wincing in pain yet smiling, kidding]

I bet you don't see stuff like that or hear those kinds of words very often in nice, old-fashioned Mennonite families. I'm sorry that you had to see that.

Lynn
[shocked and disappointed]
Oh my goodness, Dave, who was that girl and why did she say those things and do that to you?

Dave
We met at the "welcome back" picnic and she showed an interest in me. I guess she was more interested in me than I realized. But that was before I met you, and fell head over heels for you!

Lynn
[still hurt and disappointed]
No one would react like that to a guy just because they met him and showed an interest in him. What else did you do at the picnic?

Dave
[guilty and sad; stares at the ground]
We took a walk in the woods in the moonlight and we made out for a while. But she kissed me first, I didn't start it, honest, and like I said, that was long before I met you.

Lynn
[Visibly crushed and very sad; she stares downward, deeply hurt and disappointed by this news, then she looks at Dave with a completely devastated expression]
Dave, how could that have been long before you met me when the "welcome back" picnic was last weekend? We met just three days after the picnic, and our first kiss was the day after that!

[Long pause]

After I waited so long to finally be able to date someone, I feel very badly betrayed that I trusted and gave my love to someone who could go so quickly and so easily from the arms of one girl to another. I also betrayed the trust of my parents and a promise I made to them not to date until my birthday. All for a boy that wasn't really worth it. Could you please walk me back to my dorm?

Dave
[absolutely devastated and ashamed]
Yes, I'd be happy to. I'm more sorry than words can say.

Lynn
[Nods twice, very slowly and sadly, to acknowledge his words]

[They turn and begin to walk side by side in the direction of her dormitory. Their posture is one of deep disappointment and sadness, as they walk slowly without speaking. After a few steps, Dave awkwardly reaches for her hand to hold it, but Lynn feeling his touch pulls it away and puts into her pocket, as if she is recoiling from something repulsive or distasteful]

[At the front door of her dorm, she turns to enter the building without looking toward him or saying a word. Dave stops and looks after her, his eyes filling with tears]

[Fade to black]

[Two weeks later] A practice room somewhere in the music building:

Andy and Dave are playing a trumpet duet in one of the practice rooms as the afternoon sunlight streams through the open window. They are seated in two chairs, with their

backs to the piano, facing a large mirror on the opposite wall. They are playing from a book that rests on one heavy black music stand. The window is to their left and the entry door to their right.

Their complex call-and-response duet sounds impressive, as they skillfully weave a pattern of notes that overlap and complement each other beautifully. As they play the final notes, they put their trumpets on their laps and relax back into their chairs. Andy smiles with accomplishment, but Dave looks pretty down.

Andy
That wasn't too shabby for a couple of freshmen. That's a nice one. This book has a lot of good duets in it.

Dave
[down in the dumps]
Yeah, that is a nice duet; I like that one. That was fun.

Andy
Really? 'Cause you sure don't look like you're havin' any fun.

Dave
[sadly, quietly]
Lynn dropped out of college and went back home to Ohio.

[Long pause; then swallows hard]

She never really liked being here alone, so far from her family, and she always had second thoughts about whether a career in music was right for her. I guess when she started to fall in love with me she was happier, because at least she had one "loved one" here that she could count on and spend time with. But when she discovered that I was someone that she really couldn't count on, that was it. That was the last straw.

[Long pause]

I wish I had more experience with girls before I came here. I was in love with Lynn, and she could've counted on me, but now she'll never know it. I'd give anything to someday be able to marry someone as beautiful and as nice as Lynn.

Andy
Whoa, hold on there, Bucko, you're still only seventeen years old! I don't think you should even be thinkin' about marriage for quite some time. Like you said, you didn't have much experience with girls in high school. So you really have a lot of wild oats to sow **[smiles]** and I'm just the guy to help you sow them.

[continuing like a salesman] I think that a trip downtown to the bar scene this Friday is just what the doctor ordered for you, my man. You need to do something wild and crazy right now, and have a few drinks.

Dave
[shrugs, doubtful]
I dunno, I'm not much of a drinker.

Andy
You don't have to be a big drinker or get drunk; just have a couple of beers. The important thing is that the girls are drinking and they're only down there for two things:

[pauses and smiles] to have fun, and to meet guys! They aren't your sweet, innocent Mennonite girls either. A lot of them are upperclassman, and they're the kind of girls that have been around, (if you know what I mean). Most of the girls will have a few drinks so they're not nervous about meeting people. They're hoping some nice guy's gonna buy them a drink, then spend some time talking or dancing with them; later, he might even walk them back to the campus. If they like him, they might even sit out on the soccer field with him in the moonlight and talk **[elbows Dave with a smile]** . . . or maybe do more than talk, (if you know what I mean).

Dave
[nodding thoughtfully]
Yep, I have heard that the soccer field is the "makeout spot" for couples on Friday and Saturday nights.

Andy
That's right, it's the only place you can take a girl right now unless you've got a car. But they're talking about starting a new policy, called "intervisitation," next year, where a girl can go right up to a guys dorm room any time of the day or night—even spend the night if they want to! That'll be amazing if it passes!

[That Friday night] Outside a local bar on the main street of Fredonia:

It's dark as Andy and Dave cross the main street of the village in front of The Caboose bar and nightclub. As they head for the front door of the popular nightspot, they see that the entrance is an old railroad caboose. The pounding beat of loud rock music comes from within as they wait by the door to be

admitted. While they wait, several other groups of college guys and girls appear also heading for the club.

Dave

[as they wait in line]

Do you really think that phony ID you gave me is gonna work?

Andy

Don't worry; the junior who loaned it to me said it works like a charm. He uses it all the time to get his younger friends in.

[While they wait, a group of four attractive, provocatively dressed girls walk past them; both boys follow them wistfully with their eyes]

Andy

[moving his shoulders to the beat]

Wow! It looks like there are a lot of very "talented" young ladies out on the town tonight. I'm glad I talked you into coming.

Dave

I have to admit, this is kind of exciting. Don't know if I'll have the "guts" to approach some strange girl in a bar, though.

[Abrupt cut to a new scene]

[A few minutes later] Inside The Caboose bar and nightclub:

Andy and Dave push their way through a crowd of young people as they make their way toward a large room that has the bar and a dance floor. The dark room throbs with overly loud music and strobe lights of all colors flash and pulsate. The flashing lights give the dancers a jerky, robot-like appearance as they gyrate to the music of the song "Spinning Wheel" by the band Chicago.

The two boys stop in an open spot at the side of the crowded dance floor to take in the scene around them. Andy looks around, then smiles and nods at Dave with an "I told you so" kind of smile. Dave, wide-eyed and nervous, looks around the room in awe of this wild new world. He raises his eyebrows then answers with several slow nods of his own.

As they make their way to the bar, attractive, well-dressed young women are everywhere, some with guys but more often in small groups with other girls. Some girls are dancing provocatively in groups (a few even with drinks in their hands), while others sit at tables laughing and talking loudly as they sip drinks and smoke cigarettes. The guys that aren't with girls seem to be standing around the room in small groups trying to look as "cool" as possible while they "survey the scene" and plan their next move with their wingman.

Andy boldly pushes his way into an open spot at the bar. Raising his finger to get the bartender's attention, he calls out.

Andy
Can I get two drafts down here, please?

[A female bartender nods, fills two glasses, and then slides them down to Andy. Setting two dollars on the bar, he turns and hands one of them to Dave.]

Andy
Don't be afraid. If you see something you like, just go up to her and start a conversation. Ask her what her major is or where she's from. They expect guys to do that. The worse she can say is "get lost," then you just move on and try again somewhere else.

The boys stand at the edge of the dance floor, nodding and moving their heads to the music as they watch the dancers and try to get noticed by any of the girls who are dancing or the ones seated at tables. As they raise their glasses to drink, a close-up of the clock on the wall behind the bar shows that it's nine thirty.

[The hands sweep quickly around the clock's face, using time lapse photography until they stop at eleven thirty.

As the camera pulls back, we see that the two boys are still standing together in about the same spot. To hide their boredom and disappointment they're trying to look as "cool" and "with it" as they possibly can, but they're really not fooling anyone.

Dave
Looks like our glasses are empty again; I'll fill 'em this time.

[Dave pushes his way into an opening at the bar next to a blonde girl seated on a barstool. She appears to be alone as she nurses a drink and stares straight ahead into the mirror behind the bar, smoking a cigarette. We see a shot of her back and also a shot of her face in the mirror at the same time. As Dave leans in to hail the bartender, she is looking at him, using the mirror to "check him out".

Dave

Can I get a couple more drafts down here, please?

Shannon

[to Dave, while exhaling smoke]

You're a music major, aren't you? Freshman trumpet player, right?

Dave

[Surprised, smiles shyly]

Yes, I am. . Dave . . Dave Tripiciano, but how'd you know that?

Shannon

Shannon. Shannon Dougherty. I play bass clarinet in the symphonic band, and you're the first-chair trumpet. You must be really good to have that seat as a freshman.

Dave

[smiling, a little embarrassed]

Well . . . **[hesitates]** I practiced three hours a day all through high school.

Shannon

[blurts out loudly]

Three hours a day, you're kidding! When'd ya have time for girls?

Dave

I didn't. What I gained as a musician I lost in my social life.

Shannon

What a shameful waste: a guy with your looks living the life of a recluse. I bet there were some sad girls at your high school.

Dave

[matter of fact]

No, actually most of the girls at my high school thought I was a nerd. But, hey! C'mon now, I see how you knew I'm a trumpet player, but how'd you know I'm a freshman?

Shannon

[turning toward Dave, smiling]

When you've been around the college and this bar scene for as many years as I have, you can spot freshman guys a mile away. I'm a graduate assistant working on my masters in musical theater.

[As she turns toward Dave to say this, he gets a good look at her for the first time. She is older, probably in her mid-twenties, with long, unkempt, curly blonde hair. Dressed in a loose-fitting flannel shirt and jeans, she comes across as a hippie or artist type. Tall and thin, she's attractive but has a tough, hard-boiled quality about her, like a girl who's "been around." It's clear that she's had a few drinks—probably one too many. . . She spins on her bar stool, holding her cigarette in her right hand, and surveys the dance floor, nodding her head to the music]

[matter of factly] The tall guy over there's Jeremy. He's a good kisser; I gave him a nine out of ten once for a kiss that lasted two minutes. We dated for a while last year. The blonde one with the great smile is AJ. Killer looks, but very shy and unsure of himself when you get him alone. The average-looking dude dancing with two girls at once is Doug. He's not so great-lookin' and he's kinda short, but he really knows how to give a girl a good time.

[Pauses, she's a little tipsy. She puts her cigarette in an ashtray, and looks at Dave] Wanna dance, trumpet player?

Dave
[smiling]
Sure, love to.

[A couple of minutes later] The two of them slow dancing in the middle of the crowded dance floor: The girl is leaning closely into Dave and has both arms around him. She has her head resting on his shoulder as they sway slowly back and forth.

A short distance away across the floor stands Dave's buddy, Andy. As he spots Dave dancing with the attractive blonde his jaw drops and his eyes widen. While Shannon's back is to him, he waves his hand to get Dave's attention, and then he nods slowly and comically, with his mouth wide open, as he gives Dave two very eager thumbs ups.

Dave
[in Shannon's ear as they dance]
So you judge guys' kissing abilities? And give them a numerical score on how well they kiss?

Shannon
[keeps her face on his shoulder]
Yes, it's a favorite hobby of mine. The guys love it. They make a big game out of coming up to me whenever they know I've had a few drinks to see if they can get me to give them a ten, but I never give anybody a ten because then they might stop comin' back.

[Pauses]

[lifting her face to smile at him] How about you, sailor? Let's see what you got.

[Raising her face toward Dave's with a naughty smile, her lips part slightly. Dave leans in and kisses her softly yet deeply. As they kiss, the girl opens her mouth wider and moves her head back and forth as she presses her body into his. It's clear that she's had a lot of experience doing this. As she pulls away, she smiles thoughtfully as she wipes her lips with the tip of one finger]

Wow! Not bad for a freshman, not bad at all. That was at least a seven—and nobody ever gets a seven on the first try.

[Andy, who is watching all this from a distance, is beside himself with excitement. Dave and Shannon don't notice him but he is the perfect comic relief as he jumps up and down, slams the top of his head, bites then shakes his hand, and softly chants words of encouragement under his breath]

Dave
[flattered, chuckles, then kids her]
Well, I guess that's quite a compliment, coming from such a sought-after, well-respected kissing judge like you. It's getting kinda late, how about I walk you back to the campus?

Shannon
[with a knowing smile]
Sure why not, I've given lots of other guys a chance. Why not a really cute freshman who's a great trumpet player and a good kisser?

[Abrupt cut to a new scene]

Dave and Shannon walking down a village sidewalk:

Dave and Shannon are walking hand in hand toward the campus in the moonlight. Shannon, a little tipsy, laughs softly and leans into Dave playfully as they walk. It's fall, and the couple shuffles their way through a layer of dry, rustly leaves. There are also large piles of leaves along the curbside.

Dave
When I was a kid, my sisters and I loved to rake leaves into a big pile and then jump off the porch steps into them.

Shannon
Me too! It's amazing how much bigger and more exciting everything is when you're little. Sometimes I wish I could have stayed a kid forever, like Peter Pan.

Dave
[points at the stars]
Yep, "Second star to the right and straight on till morning."

Shannon
[a sly tone, as if she's got something up her sleeve]
Speaking of stars, why don't we cut across the soccer field on our way back to my dorm? That's my favorite place to sit and look up at the moon and stars on a beautiful night like this. If we turn right on that sidewalk up there, we'll come right to it.

[Abrupt cut to a new scene]

Dave and Shannon walking across the soccer field in the dark:

Shannon points to the sky as the two of them walk slowly across the dark athletic field. Both of them are looking up at the stars as they talk, pointing out different constellations.

Shannon
[Kneels and then pulls Dave by the hand to kneel next to her on the grass]

[points] That's the Big Dipper. There's something about drawing a line through two of the stars in the dipper and then if you follow it across the sky it points to the North Star, but I can't remember.

Dave
It's the two stars that form the front of the bowl of the dipper. Those two right there. **[points]** Draw a line through them and follow it up; it takes you right to the North Star.

[As soon as he finishes the words "North Star" and looks at her, Shannon covers his lips with her open mouth and begins kissing him aggressively. Still kissing, they rise to an erect kneeling position with their arms around each other and their bodies facing each other. Their passionate embrace creates an artistic silhouette right below the full moon as the long kiss continues.

As the kiss ends, Shannon reclines onto her back on the grass in a position of surrender. With a naughty smile, she reaches up to grab the front of Dave's shirt and pulls him down on top of her. Again, she begins to kiss him deeply with an open mouth.

[Fade to black]

[New scene]

The sidewalk in front of Shannon's dorm entrance:

Dave is holding her hand as he walks Shannon down the sidewalk to her dorm. They stop and face each other at the point where the sidewalk to the front entrance T's into the main sidewalk. Dave has a smile, but Shannon, now sobering up, seems less warm, more businesslike, and not as playful as before. There's an awkward silence as they shuffle their feet for a moment.

Shannon
That was nice, Dave; I'm glad I met you and got to have some fun with you tonight. You're a very nice guy, and I know you're gonna do very well with the girls here. Because you are just a freshman and I'm a graduate assistant, I have to be careful to protect my reputation. It would mean a lot to me if this becomes nothing more than a memory and a well-kept secret. Please don't tell anyone about tonight, especially here at the college, okay?

Dave
[nods in agreement; then tries to cover his disappointment by acting cool and casual]
Sure, oh absolutely. We had a fun night and we've got a great memory that'll stay just between us (crosses his heart) I promise.

Shannon
[winks]
If we see each other around campus or downtown, we'll just pretend like we're total strangers; then no one will ever know, okay?

Dave
[forces a smile and agrees]
Whatever you say, you're the "babe", and I had fun with you.

Shannon
[relieved, placating]
Thanks Dave, you really are a nice guy for a freshman. Well, good night, and thanks again for walkin' me back.

[Dave leans in and puts an arm around her back, hoping to at least get a goodnight kiss. But she quickly pulls back, ducks her head to the right, and gives him a quick peck on the cheek. Then flashing him a plastic smile, she whirls around and scampers down the sidewalk, up the steps, and out of sight through the entry doors, without ever looking back or saying another word. Dave, shocked, stands there looking sadly after her, as he tries to understand and process what just happened]

[Fade to black]

Act 6 •

Friends With Benefits Or A Serious Girlfriend?

[Several weeks later] A symphonic band rehearsal, in the music building:

The band is playing a difficult, up-tempo piece, with great skill and musicianship. Lynn's chair is gone from the flute section and Shannon is playing the bass clarinet. Dave and Andy are again sitting at the far left end of the trumpet section.

The conductor waves his arms then raises his right hand high in the air to bring the music to a sudden and abrupt stop. Directing his gaze and pointing his baton at two female trumpet players, seated all the way at the other end of the line of trumpets from Dave, he speaks:

Conductor
Third trumpets, my dear third trumpets; Vicki and Kate, is it?

Kate
[shyly]
Yes sir, Vicki and Kate, Dr. Greenwood.

Conductor
Now girls, there's a time to be polite, feminine, and ladylike, and there's a time to be a BRASS PLAYER **[he says "brass player" in a**

loud, harsh, powerful voice to emphasize the words strongly; as he does, some giggles and whispers go through the group, and Andy looks at Dave with a knowing smile]

Conductor

There are no "small" parts or less important parts in a band.

The third trumpet part must be played with the same kind of power and confidence as the first trumpet part. If anything, it actually needs to be played with more power since acoustically low sounds do not project as well or cut through a band the way that high sounds do.

Ladies, I encourage you to be as shy as you want to when a young man you don't know tries to buy you a drink downtown, but please don't be shy with that third trumpet part at number thirty-seven.

Andy

[To Dave]

Like I always said: shy girl, shy sound.

Dave

[To Andy, joking]

There ought'a be a law against letting a girl play the trumpet.

[Dave didn't mean to, but he said this last remark much louder than he should have, and many of the female faces in the room snap quickly in his direction with angry expressions. Vicki and Kate both make a terrible face at Dave, and Kate even sticks her tongue out at him. The conductor is amused and can't resist this opportunity to make a joke and a comment]

Conductor

[smiling]

I would be very careful, Mr. Tripiciano, about making comments like that in these days of Women's Lib. We don't want to find you covered with tar and feathers and hanging from a streetlight.

[A ripple of laughter passes through the room; as things settle down and the players stop looking at Dave, rehearsal continues]

Conductor

Alright ladies and gentlemen, let's start at twenty, and I want to hear some real confidence and power from the third trumpets at number thirty-seven.

[He raises his hands to start the group, but has another thought and puts them down. He pauses then speaks with a wry smile]

[To Dave] Since you found it necessary to make an insulting remark to Vicki and Kate during rehearsal today, I feel that a true gentleman would make up for it by offering to give them a couple of private lessons. You can tutor them in a practice room, at any time that is mutually convenient, on how to play with more power. Don't think of it as punishment, but as teaching experience and a nice way to apologize.

[There's some murmuring, some laughing, and some giggling; as some of the band members look back at Dave again smiling]

Kate

[to Vicki, madder than a wet hen]

I wouldn't let that cocky, arrogant, male chauvinist tutor me if he was the last trumpet teacher in the world.

Vicki

[quietly to Kate]

Oh, just relax will you! It might be kind of fun and we might even learn something. Besides, he's a cute boy and we haven't had many of those going out of their way to meet us since we got here.

Conductor

Once again now, start at twenty and I want to hear some power from the third trumpets at thirty-seven. One, two, ready, and . . .

[The band begins to play again and the conductor directs with much vigor. We see him signal Vicki and Kate for more power and the girls respond by blowing with a lot of energy. Dave and Andy raise their eyebrows, looking to their right and nodding while playing, as they finally hear the third trumpets]

[Abrupt cut to a new scene]

The crowded hallway outside the band room right after band practice:

Kate and Vicki stand in the hallway talking, as Vicki puts her trumpet case into a storage locker. Dave walks up to them, carrying his trumpet case. Kate assumes a very cold, angry expression as he approaches, but Vicki greets him with a smile.

Dave
[apologetically]
I'm really sorry, guys. I said that to Andy just kidding around and trying to be a comedian in front of the guys. I didn't mean for you girls to hear it, and I don't really believe it either.

Vicki
[flirting]
That's okay; we know you were just trying to be funny.

Kate
[softening a little]
Well, it's really not okay, and it wasn't a bit funny, but it does mean a lot that you took the time to stop and say you're sorry.

Dave
Dr. Greenwood is usually an old fuddy-duddy, but I think he had a great idea this time. What better way could there be for me to make it up to you than to give you a couple of lessons. It'll help me become a better teacher, too. Lots of guys think that girl brass players don't play with enough guts, but if you think about it, many of the best wind players in the major symphony orchestras are females.

Vicki
[smiling eagerly]
I'd like that, Dave. I think it would be kind of fun.

Kate
[softening more]
Well, I guess a couple of sessions wouldn't hurt. Maybe we can play some duets and trios. As long as you don't rub it in that you're the "big shot" first-chair trumpet, and we're just the wimpy, girl third trumpets.

Dave
[graciously]
I'd never do that. I'm at your service, and happy to help.

[Abrupt cut to a new scene]

An upstairs practice room in the music building:

Dave is standing in front of Kate and Vicki, who are seated in chairs facing him. Dave is holding his trumpet and they have their trumpets on their laps as they listen to him intently. Vicki is a large, chubby girl with short hair. Most guys would probably find her unappealing. She's shy, loveable, and everybody's friend, and she dreams of one day finding a boyfriend. Kate is a tall, thin girl with medium-length brown hair. A "plain Jane" with the kind of looks that some boys would find appealing.

Dave
[sincerely trying to help]
The only difference between powerful, aggressive players and weaker players is that the strong players take in a tremendous amount of air and then push it through their instrument using their stomach muscles and diaphragm. You have to use the same muscles to push the air out as the ones you use to push stuff out when you go to the bathroom.

[At this, both girls smile at each other and start to giggle]

Dave
C'mon now, give it a try. Take a huge breath, push some air through those things, and give me the loudest, fullest C scale you've ever played. **[loudly, like a coach]** I don't ever again want to hear anyone say that my "girls" don't play with guts.

[The girls take a deep breath and start to play a loud, strong scale]

[Fade to black]

[Two days later, in the evening] In the same practice room:

Dave is alone in the room, sitting at the piano with his trumpet on his lap. He is absent-mindedly plunking out a simple one-finger melody on the keys as he waits for the girls. The door opens and Kate enters shyly with her trumpet case. [She is alone]

Dave
Hi Kate, how's it going? Ready for your lesson?

Kate
[as she takes her trumpet out]
Yes, I'm ready. I hate to admit it, but some of the things you showed us really have helped my playing. You're a good teacher and very nice, and you seem to be sincerely interested in helping us. I really wasn't expecting you to be like that, but it means a lot. Thank you. [pause] I'm sorry I was kinda angry and mean that day in band.

Dave
No problem, I'm enjoying helping you guys. Where's Vicky?

Kate
It's just gonna be me tonight. Vicky's been really sick all day.

Dave
Okay, maybe we'll just play some duets and work on sight-reading.

[Dave stands and begins to flip through a pile of music books on the piano; as he does, he questions Kate]

Dave
So, where you from Kate? I don't know much about ya.

Kate
[sitting with her trumpet]
I'm a country girl. I grew up on a farm in Old Forge, a small town in the Adirondacks. We get lots of snow up there in the winter.

Dave
That's a beautiful area. My parents took us there on vacation when we were kids.

[Finds the book he wants, flops it onto the music stand, and sits next to her, flipping through the book]

Dave
Let's see now, here's a good one, number thirty-eight: easy and fun to play, yet impressive sounding. It's by Mozart, too! You're going to have to count really good to play this one, Kate.

[While Dave is digging for the duet book, asking about her hometown, picking out a duet, and encouraging her, Kate watches him with a soft smile and admiring eyes. It's clear that she's beginning to have feelings for him]

Dave
Ready? Okay, here we go: one, two, ready, and . . .

[They begin to play the duet, sounding full and impressive as they trade overlapping phrases back and forth. As they reach the end of the piece they put their trumpets down, smiling]

Dave

That a girl! Nice job Kate! That was great playing!

Kate

[shy, embarrassed]

Aw — c'mon, you're just sayin' that.

Dave

No I'm not, I'm very proud of you. **[Pauses, thinks a moment, laughs inwardly and then continues]** As a matter of fact, I can tell people honestly that you're the best trumpet student I've ever had! **[Then bringing his hand to the side of his mouth, he adds a side comment under his breath in the style of Groucho Marx].** Of course, I won't tell them that you're the only trumpet student I've ever had.

Kate

[Laughing, Kate leans into Dave and elbows him playfully] What a joker you are; you're such a joker and a tease.

[She stops laughing and gets suddenly serious. Her voice and facial expression soften and change to one of admiration and affection. As she turns to face him, she leans in close to stare into his eyes]

Kate

But you really are a nice guy, a very nice guy, and I love the way you help and encourage me.

[At this point her face is just twelve inches from his. As she moves even closer her eyelids droop, she raises her chin and opens her mouth slightly. Dave, surprised and pleased, gets the message and moves in to kiss her softly on the mouth. With

their trumpets on their laps, seated in slightly awkward positions, they lock lips in a very long, very tender kiss. Each has one hand on their trumpet and the other hand behind the head of the person they are kissing.

[Fade to black]

[Two hours later] Kate's dorm room. Kate is talking on the phone:

Kate
[smiling, very excited]
No, I'm not kidding Vicky, I kissed Dave in a practice room while we were practicing and he kissed me back! It was like a scene from a soap opera!

Vicky
How exciting, I guess it was lucky for you that I was sick for the past couple of days, because you got to be alone with him.

Kate
It was very beautiful, we kissed for a while then we talked for a long time, then we kissed some more. Then he walked me back to my dorm and kissed me goodnight. I think I'm kind of his girlfriend now.

Vicky
You lucky dog! I'm very happy for you Kate, way to go!

Kate
He wants to take me to a movie at the theater downtown tomorrow and then go to the Caboose to have a couple of drinks. He also said we can stop and sit on the soccer field to look at the moon and stars on the way back if it's a nice night. Isn't that romantic?

Vicky
Uh, oh! You be careful young lady. If he wants to sit out there with you, he might be hoping to do more than just look at the moon and stars. The soccer field is the place where couples go on weekends to do a lot more than just kiss, if you get my drift.

Kate
[scared yet excited]
You think so? I've never gone that far with a boy before.

Vicky
I know, and you shouldn't be too eager to give it away to the first boy you date in college. You need to save it for someone special: the guy that you really believe is "the one."

Kate
Thanks Vick, I'll try to be wise and go slow, but he is good-looking and very nice. I think I might be falling in love.

Vicky
Well, just be careful and remember that I'm gonna want details, lots and lots of details.

Kate
[smiles]
I'll take notes so you don't miss a thing, how's that?

Vicky
[also smiles]
Perfect! Love ya, have a great time, and call me Saturday.

[Abrupt cut to a new scene]

A series of short vignettes (with no dialogue, just musical background) show Dave and Kate dating, having fun, and spending time together, as their relationship continues over the next five or six months:

[Background music only, throughout]

Vignette #1: Dave and Kate are in a movie theater, smiling and watching a movie together as they share a bag of popcorn and a cold drink. He has his arm around her as the light from the screen flickers on their faces.

Vignette #2: They are in the same local bar that Dave was in earlier when he met Shannon. Kate smiles up at him as they slow dance; then she leans her cheek down against his shoulder. She smiles contentedly.

Vignette #3: They are sitting on the soccer field on a beautiful moonlit night. Dave has his arm around her as he points out stars in the sky. Looking up she nods, smiles, and then they kiss tenderly.

Vignette #4: They're in a practice room playing duets. Dave stops them, shaking his head; then he points to something in the music, correcting and teasing her. She slugs him playfully, then they both laugh and then hug.

Vignette #5: A symphonic band rehearsal. The band is playing and the conductor artistically shapes the music with his arms and hands. The trumpet section is playing with a lot of energy. Dave's eyes suddenly widen with surprise as he hears something that impresses him. He turns to look down the line and gives Kate a big smile and a thumbs up. Smiling at him, she puts her trumpet down and flexes her arm muscle.

[March of their freshman year] Inside a student dining hall:

Dave, Kate, and Vicky are seated at a table, eating dinner from cafeteria-style trays. Andy appears, hurrying toward them with a smile and carrying a heavily laden tray of food. He has a briefcase-style book bag slung over his shoulder, which he drops on the far end of their table; then plops down in the chair next to Dave. He's grinning from ear to ear, and quite excited about the big news he's heard.

Andy
You're not gonna believe it. You guys are not going to believe it, but it's true; they finally did it!

Dave
What are you talking about? I've never seen you so excited.

Andy
Intervisitation, man: intervisitation! I can't believe that a guy with a steady girlfriend hasn't been following these developments! After years of haggling back and forth, this old fashioned, traditional, conservative college finally passed the policy of intervisitation. That means that a girl is allowed to be in a guy's dorm room at any time of the day or night and vice versa!

Vicky
No way! That means that a girl or a guy can sleep in their boyfriend or girlfriend's room whenever they want to!

Kate
[shrugs]
Well, it doesn't mean that a couple has to sleep together. They can watch TV, study, and just spend quality time together.

Dave
[thoughtfully]
Wow, that is hard to believe. When does it start?

Andy
Next Saturday, and the soccer field will be like a barren, forgotten, uninhabited, deserted wasteland from that day on.

[Fade to black]

[The following Saturday] In the lounge of Dave's dorm building:

Standing around the room and sitting on the couches and chairs of the downstairs TV lounge are a dozen couples. Dave and Kate are there, leaning against the back of a sofa talking. A few of the boys and girls keep glancing at the clock at the far end of the room, as if they're waiting for something. It's 4:30 in the afternoon. A handsome, dark-haired young man is standing near the center of the room, while his girlfriend, a short cute girl with dirty blonde hair, is holding his hand and leaning her body against his, almost as if they're dancing. She has her face resting on his shoulder. He speaks:

Dark-Haired Boy
[In New York City accent]
Thirty more minutes, gentlemen. In thirty more minutes you'll be a part of history, as you escort your girlfriend up to your room. This momentous occasion marks the first time ever that girls will be allowed to go upstairs in a boy's dormitory at Fredonia State.

[Abrupt cut to a new scene]

[Thirty-five minutes later] In an upstairs hallway of the dorm:

Dave and Kate are walking down a corridor, past the numbered doors of student rooms. They pass another couple coming toward them in the narrow hallway then round a corner and come to a stop at the door of Dave's room. He fumbles for the key in his pocket as Kate stands nervously behind him. As he unlocks the door, he speaks:

Dave
This is gonna be great! My roommate's from Jamestown and he went home for the weekend, so we've got the place all to ourselves!

Kate
[agreeing, but still a little nervous]
That's great . . . I – I Guess.

[The door swings open and Dave happily motions with his hand for her to go in. He tries to put on a phony "French accent" as he speaks]

Dave
[motioning graciously]
Après vous, mademoiselle! I think that means, "after you, young lady!"

Kate
[smiling, playing along]
Why thank you, sir. What lovely accommodations you have here in Paris.

They enter the room and the door closes behind them.

[Fade to black]

[The next afternoon] In Kate's dorm room:

Kate is alone in her room, talking on the telephone with Vicky.

Kate
I spent the night in his room and we slept together. **[Pauses—the next part is hard for her to say—then she blurts out]** And . . . and . . . we did it, we went all the way.

Vicky
Well, I pretty much expected that would happen with the intervisitation thing coming in. What was it like?

Kate
Actually, it kind of hurt a little and it wasn't really as magical or as beautiful as I dreamed it would be. It meant a lot to him though, and it was really nice having him hold me all night. I really wanted to do it, or at least I thought I did. But now I just feel kind of confused, guilty, and embarrassed.

Vicky

[sympathetic, understanding]

Don't feel bad. I've heard that the first time can be disappointing and very emotional for nice girls who were brought up right. But it's supposed to get better with time and practice, and can be very beautiful between two married people who are deeply in love. Let's just hope that will be you two someday, and that this is just the beginning of the story where you guys live happily ever after.

Kate

[smiling happily]

You're the best Vick. Where'd I ever get a friend like you?

Vicky

I just hope he feels the same way about you as you do about him Kate, and that you're not investing your heart and soul in the wrong guy and setting yourself up for a huge disappointment. Summer vacation's coming up pretty soon, ya know. What're you gonna do then?

Kate

[excited, eager]

Actually, we talked about that last night too. He's coming to Old Forge in July to meet my parents and spend a few days at my house. Then I'm gonna go to his house, and do the same in August!

Vicky

That sounds great, if it really happens. I hope all this works out to be better than a dream come true for you. Love ya, bye!

[Fade to black]

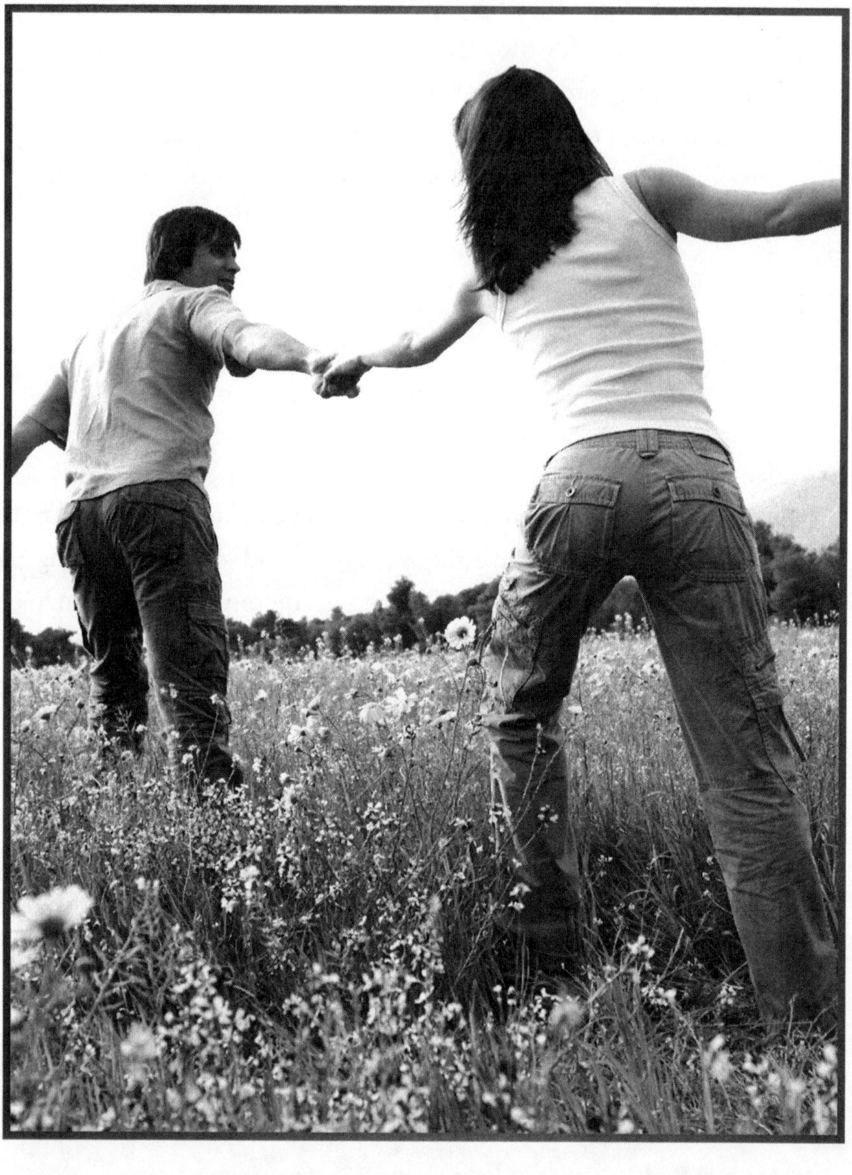

Act 7 •
Summer Vacation And Meeting The Parents

The kitchen of Kate's parent's home in Old Forge, New York:

Kate's mom is at the stove cooking while her dad looks over her shoulder, sniffing what's in the pot. Her dad is middle-aged, gray-haired, and solidly built. Her mom is slender, with glasses and gray hair; she has the classic look of a farm wife. They are down-to-earth, hard-working country people with good hearts and the wisdom of age.

Kate's Dad
So what did you say this guy's name is?

Kate's Mom
Dave, Dave Trip-i-ci-ano **[badly mispronounces his last name]**

Kate's Dad
Holy cow, that's *Italian,* isn't it? When I was in the service the Italian guys were the big womanizers. They were always flirting with the girls and seemed to have a different girlfriend every week.

Kate's Mom
Now, now, Kate says he's very nice and he's been helping her a lot with her trumpet. Most importantly, I think your daughter's falling in love with him; so you just be nice, understand?

[He reaches into the pot, but she slaps his hand away]

[Abrupt cut to a new scene]

An older car driving down a country road, with Dave at the wheel:

Dave, driving, spots a small, rundown family farm on the right. The well-worn roadside mailbox has the name Morgan on it so he smiles, nods, and turns into the driveway. Three chickens scurry away from his car as he pulls across the barnyard, and Kate comes bounding down the porch steps with a smile, waving eagerly as she runs to greet him.

As he steps from the car she almost tackles him, as she reaches him and they embrace. She is dressed casually in a flannel shirt and jeans, and looks very much like a country girl. Then pulling him by the hand, she leads him eagerly toward the house.

[Abrupt cut to a new scene]

Inside the kitchen, Kate's mom and dad are standing at the stove:

Kate enters eagerly, with a big smile, proudly pulling Dave by the hand behind her. Her mom smiles graciously as he enters, and crosses the room to meet him; while her dad hangs back at first.

Kate
[smiling proudly]
This is Dave, my friend from college.

Kate's Mom
It's nice to meet you Dave, we've sure heard a lot about you.

Dave
Very nice to meet you ma'am. Kate's a very nice girl.

Kate's Dad
[crossing to shake hands]
Good meetin' you young man. Welcome to the north country. Kate says you've been helping her quite a bit with her trumpet.

Dave
[smiling]
Well, I've been teasing her a lot about girl trumpet players, and I guess I finally got her mad enough to play with some fire power.

Kate's Mom
You just make yourself at home Dave. Dinners not till six, so you've got several hours and it's a beautiful day. Maybe Kate can give you a guided tour of the farm, the woods and our pond.

Dave
That would be great! I'm an outdoorsman and I love the country.

[Abrupt cut to a new scene]

[Thirty minutes later] Dave and Kate are swimming in a hidden pond located back in the woods. Only their heads are visible above water as they swim, laugh, and splash each other playfully.

All of their clothes are in two piles on a towel in the grass, including all their underwear and their shoes, so it's clear that they're "skinny dipping" in the pond.

Dave
[smiling]
This is pretty cool. When you asked me to go for a swim and I said I didn't bring a bathing suit, I had no idea that this is what you had in mind. You're pretty naughty and spontaneous for a sweet, wholesome, country girl.

Kate
[laughing]
Just because you're a good trumpet player, doesn't mean you know how to have fun on a hot summer day. We better get out before the snapping turtles figure out there's a naked boy in the pond.

Dave
[wide-eyed]
Snapping turtles!! Whoa!! **[Runs frantically toward shore]**

[Abrupt cut to a new scene]

[A few minutes later] Dave and Kate are lying on a towel on the grass, kissing deeply in the summer sunshine. Only their heads, necks, and the tops of their bare shoulders are visible. Dave is on top of her, as they kiss passionately.

[Fade to black]

[Three weeks later] In the kitchen of Dave's parent's home in Auburn, New York:

Dave's mother, father, and grandfather sit at the kitchen table, waiting for Dave to arrive with Kate. They are talking as they wait:

Dave's Mother
[judgmental]
What's her name? Kate Morgan? That doesn't sound very Italian.

Dave's Father
[hopeful]
I'm just happy he's finally got a real, live, serious girlfriend —and a college girl, too! - Things are lookin' up.

Grandpa DeNiro
If I were a guy his age in college right now, I'd have lots of girlfriends—not just one. Hope she's pretty.

The door opens and in walks Dave, leading Kate by the hand. He is smiling broadly as she looks down shyly, a little self-conscious about meeting Dave's family. His grandfather rises to greet the couple, giving Dave a bear hug.

Grandpa DeNiro
[hugging Dave]
Way, college Joe, how ya doin'? So the big shot college guy brings home a pretty college girl to meet the family?

[Pausing, he smiles at Kate, looking her up and down]

[continues] This must be Kate; you're a beautiful girl!

Kate
[Smiling, she blushes a deep shade of pink; she's very flattered]

Dave's Mother
[rising to shake hands]
Hi Kate, I'm Dave's mother. Very nice to meet you!

Dave's Father
[remaining seated]
Hello Kate. I'm his dad. You seem like a very nice young lady.

Dave
Since Kate's only staying for a couple of days, I thought I'd take her for a ride and show her the city of Auburn. Then maybe we'll get an ice cream and catch a movie. I'll show her the guest room and the bathroom later. Is that okay, mom? **[His mother nods her approval; then Dave turns to exit]** We won't be out very late! Thanks guys, bye, love you!

Kate
[exits after him, with a smile and a wave]
Very nice meeting all of you! We'll see you later.

Mom, Dad, and Grandpa
[all together (ad lib]
Bye, bye guys, bye Kate, nice meeting you Kate, good meeting you, drive safe, be careful [etc.]

[Fade to black]

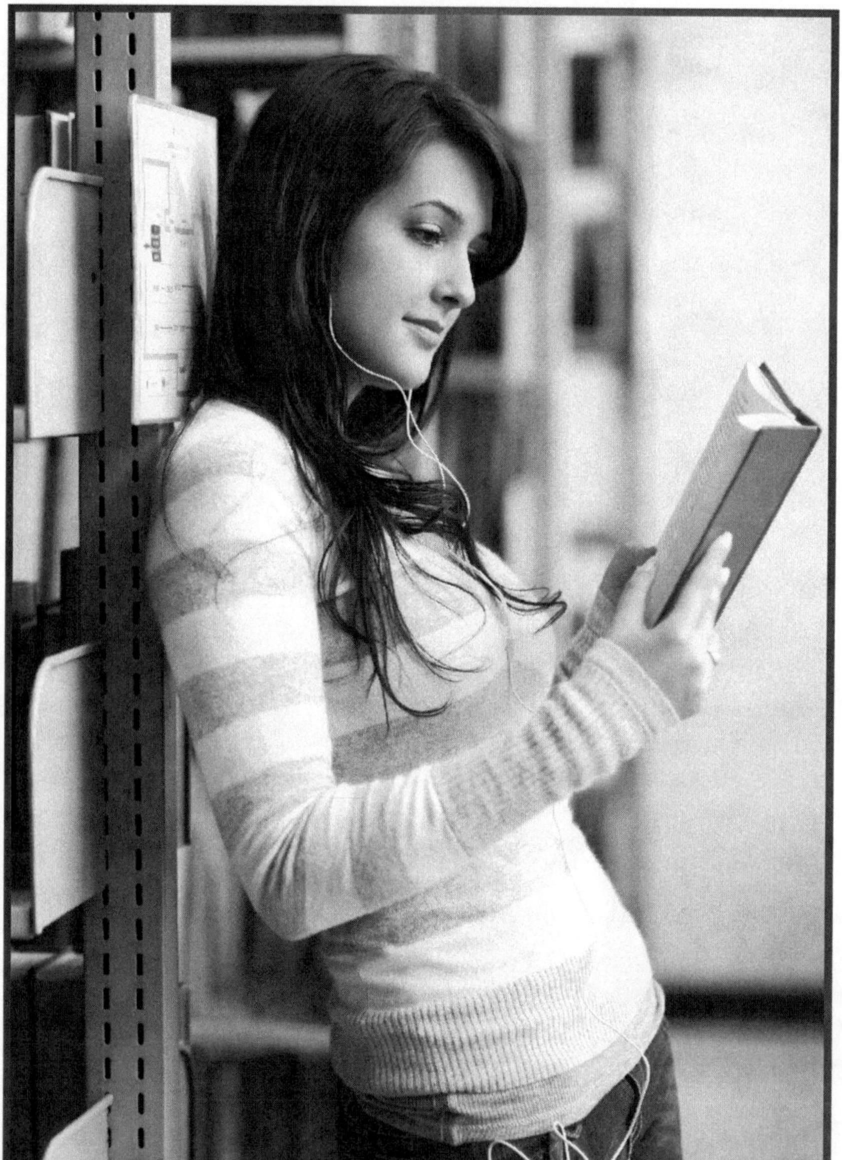

Act 8 •

A Fickle Heart And A Sucker For A Pretty Face

[September of 1970] The Fredonia College "welcome back" picnic:

Students arrive carrying blankets, coolers, and Frisbees. They enter the park through the parking lot, passing under a large banner that reads: "Welcome Back SUNY Fredonia Students."

In the crowd of students moving into the picnic area are Dave and Kate, holding hands and carrying a blanket. They're accompanied by Vicky, Andy, and several other symphonic band members.

Dave
Well, here we are guys, back at the old bandstand for another year of fun and hard work. Did you guys have a good summer? Kate and I did. She got to meet my parents, and I got to meet hers.

Andy
[teasing]
Meeting parents! Oh no! You guys must be getting pretty serious.

[Kate, smiling, elbows Andy in the ribs and then flashes Dave a smile]

Vicky
Shut up Andy, you clown, you're just jealous because they've been going together for almost a year and you're still the lone wolf.

[Four quick vignettes without dialogue, only background music]: Show Dave, Kate, and their friends having fun and enjoying themselves at the "welcome back" picnic.

[Background music only, throughout]

Vignette #1: Dave, Kate, and the gang getting food at the chef tables, putting mustard on hot dogs, dishing out salads, etc., then sitting at tables laughing, talking, teasing, eating and drinking together.

Vignette #2: Dave, Kate, Andy, and another male band member are tossing a Frisbee back and forth. Andy (always the show-off) clowns around, catching it behind his back and between his legs. Then we see Dave and Kate frantically hopping along in a three-legged race against other couples. Just as they are taking the lead, they fall to the ground laughing hysterically and tickling each other, as their friends look on laughing and pointing.

Vignette #3: It's dark and the bonfire roars and crackles. Dave and Kate are snuggled up in the front row, smiling and cuddling with their blanket wrapped around them as the firelight flickers on their faces.

Vignette #4: Dave and Kate are walking hand in hand down the corridor of Dave's dormitory. They round the corner and kiss as they come to a stop outside Dave's room. He fumbles for the key and then unlocks the door. The door opens and they enter the room, quietly closing the door behind them.

[Fade to black]

[**Two weeks later**] In the music building, at Andy's locker:

Band rehearsal has just ended and Andy is putting his instrument away in his storage locker as Dave walks up to him carrying his.

Dave
Hey man, are you doing anything right now?

Andy
No not really, I'm pretty much free until music history.

Dave
I had to special order one of my textbooks last week because they were out of them and I got a message yesterday that it came in. You wanna take a walk over to the bookstore with me?

Andy
Sure, why not. I need to walk off a big breakfast anyway.

[Abrupt cut to a new scene]

Andy and Dave in the college bookstore, browsing up and down the aisles:

Dave
Let's look through these used books for a while. Sometimes you can find something really good for just a couple of bucks. Then I can pick up the book I ordered at the counter on the way out.

Andy
Fine with me, it sure beats sitting around killing time.

[The boys work their way down toward the end of an aisle, where Dave comes across a book that contains large, colorful maps of the seas, oceans, rivers, and continents of the world]

Dave
[in awe]
Wow! Andy, look at this! Here's a book that has beautiful maps of all the oceans, waterways and countries of the world.

Andy

[mocking, sarcastic]

Wowsers! What a find!! Why in the world would I care about that?

Dave

Have you ever sailed a boat, Andy?

Andy

Yeah sure, my dad's got a twenty-foot runabout that we ski behind.

Dave [dreamily, inspired]

No, I mean sailed a boat, using just sails and the wind? I have, and it's one of the most beautiful, relaxing things in the world.

[Pauses, flips to a map of the great lakes and begins to point things out to Andy while talking excitedly]

Did you know that you can start from Fredonia, New York, right here on Lake Erie . . . **[points at a map in the book]** and sail all the way through the Great Lakes to Chicago! Then when you get there you can sail right through the center of the city and follow a river all the way down to the Mississippi! If you let the boat have her way, the current and the wind will take you to St. Louis, where you can spend a few days playing the blues with the local boys. From there, keep going down the river for several more days and you'll be in New Orleans. Then you can stay for a while and play some Dixieland jazz with the guys on Bourbon Street. Then if you're really adventurous, like me, you can set sail along the Gulf Coast, following the shoreline to Tampa and Key West, Florida. I bet you didn't know that from the Florida Keys there's a waterway that takes you all the way up the East Coast and almost to New York City without ever going out in the ocean. Did ya?

[Andy, amazed that Dave knows all this and is so excited about it; is dumfounded. He stares blankly at Dave with surprise, and simply shakes his head back and forth to say "no, he didn't know that"]

If you make it to the Big Apple, you can play in a pit orchestra on Broadway for a few nights, then sail up the Hudson River against the current all the way to Albany. From Albany, you can keep heading north through Lake Champlain and French Canada to the St. Lawrence River. Then come down through the Thousand Islands to Lake Ontario and Lake Erie. **Or** you can put your mast down in Albany, turn left, and motor all the way down the Erie Canal to Buffalo and Lake Erie. Pretty cool, huh! I bet you didn't know that you can make a complete circle of the eastern half of the United States in a boat, did you?

[Andy shakes his head again to say he didn't know that either]

[Dave continues passionately] Wouldn't it be amazing to sail from Florida to the Bahamas; and live on your boat for a year or two! It's only seventy miles! Just a one-day sail!

Or imagine how it would be to have your boat tied up at a port in Greece, and travel back and forth between harbors in Greece, Italy, the French Riviera, and Northern Africa! Living on your boat for a week or two in each port along the way!

That's why I like looking at maps and charts of the world, Andy. I love looking at them and dreaming about the places I would sail to someday, on an amazing, once-in-a-lifetime adventure!

Young Woman's Voice
[piping up out of nowhere]
Take me with you!!

[Dave, surprised, grabs Andy's arm as they look at each other wide-eyed with their mouths open]

Dave
[looking all around]
Who said that? Who said that, and where are you?

Young Woman
Right here, on the other side of the bookshelf.

[Dave carefully pulls three fat books out of the shelf and finds himself looking into the smiling face of an attractive young woman]

Young Woman
[smiling, joking playfully]
If you really do all that someday, take me with you!

[Dave is bewitched by her looks, her smile, her playfulness, and the way she talks to him like she already knows him. He tries to be cool, even though he's already been shot by Cupid's arrow]

Dave
[smiling, flirting]
Do you always listen in on other people's conversations?

Young Woman
I couldn't help but overhear since I'm standing right on the other side of the books from you. What you were saying sounded so romantic and amazing that I found myself being drawn into your dream and wanting to go to all of those places with you!

[She walks quickly around the end of the book shelf, smiling with her hand extended to introduce herself. She is short, thin, and petite, with long, straight brown hair and a strikingly pretty face. Dressed a little like a flower child, she carries herself well and has the looks and manner of a pixie or sprite]

Young Woman
[shaking hands with both boys]
Laura, Laura Malone. I'm a junior in elementary education.

Dave
[smiling]
I'm Dave and this is Andy, we're sophomores—a couple of trumpet players majoring in music and hoping to be school band directors some day. I'm from Auburn and he's from Long Island.

Laura
[all smiles]
I'm a "townie." I grew up right here in Dunkirk, just a little more than a mile from the college. Good old "Polish" Dunkirk. I was looking at the Haiku poetry on the other side of the bookshelf. Have you ever read any Haikus? I love them.

[Opens the book she is holding to show them] It's Japanese poetry that only uses three short lines to paint a word picture. Here's one look: **[points and reads]** *The red blossom bends and drips it's dew to the ground. Like a tear it falls.* Isn't that nice? Very simple, yet very beautiful.

Dave

Yes, that is pretty; I never knew poetry could be so short.

Andy

[always clowning]

Poetry that even I'd like: real short (the shorter the better)!

Laura [laughs]

Well anyway, I'm sorry for eavesdropping. Like I said, I heard you going on about sailing and seeing the world by boat, and I just had to meet the guy who was talking like that. I've always had a thing for sensitive dreamers who are really passionate about something and also adventurous. Besides, sailboats are so beautiful; do you have one?

Dave

No, but my dream is to someday own one big enough to live in.

Laura

[smiles and touches his arm]

There you go dreamin' again Dave. You're quite a guy.

[Dave looks at her hand as she touches him. It's clear that he's excited by and attracted to this pretty, petite, outgoing young woman. Sensing that the conversation is about to end, he blurts out an invitation in the hopes of seeing her again]

Dave
[hopeful]
If you're not doing anything tonight, maybe we can get together at the student union and I could treat you to coffee or an ice cream sundae, and we could talk some more?

Laura
That would be nice; I'd like that Dave, how about 8:00?

Dave
[surprised and thrilled]
Great! I'll see you then, meet me inside the front entrance.

Laura
[Smiling]
Ok – see you then!

[Abrupt cut to a new scene]

[Moments later]
Along the sidewalk between the bookstore and the music building:

Dave and Andy are on a campus sidewalk heading back to the music building. Dave carries a package as Andy speaks to him in a loud, excited voice. He is frustrated and upset as he questions Dave about asking the attractive, outgoing, older girl for a date.

Andy
Are you out of your mind!! You would have to be out of your freaking mind and have no heart at all, to ask that girl out just like that, without batting an eye, as though you were single!

Dave

Aw — come on, give me a break, will you? You saw her; she was as pretty as Lynn. Small, petite and perky like a pixie . . . with a beautiful smile and a great personality. It was as if Tinkerbelle let her hair down, dyed it brown, and became a real, live girl. On top of all that, the thing that really made her impossible to resist was the fact that she was interested in me, and seemed to really like me!

Andy

What are you going to tell Kate? You've been going together for almost a year, and you went to meet her parents, for God's sake!

Dave [feeling a little guilty]

I know, I know. . . . Most likely nothing will ever come of this, other than the memory of havin' coffee one night with one of the hottest girls on campus. But if I don't do it, I'll always wish I had; and I'll always feel like I may have missed one of the greatest opportunities in my life. Kate doesn't need to know yet; please don't tell her. Let's just see what happens and I'll deal with telling her later, if I need to. Besides, Mr. "you've got a lot of wild oats to sow and I'm just the one to help." Didn't you tell me that once? Or was that some other wild and crazy guy?

Andy

Awright, you win, but I think you're doing the wrong thing.

[Abrupt cut to a new scene]

Inside the student union snack bar/cafeteria:
Dave and Laura are seated at a small table, laughing and talking as they eat ice cream sundaes together.

Dave

I had the feeling you'd be the kind of girl who'd want an ice cream sundae rather than coffee. You seem very young for your age.

Laura

[smiling]

Well, I am pretty short and petite. My dad's Italian like you, and he's short. My mom's tall, thin, and not Italian. I guess I got my dad's height. - But good things come in small packages! **[Laughs]**

Dave

After you finish your ice cream, we can take a walk up to my dorm room, if you want. Believe it or not, I have a hamster that lives in the bottom drawer of my desk. You might get a kick out of him if you like cute, cuddly little animals. His name's Ben.

Laura

[laughs]

Oh my goodness, you are full of surprises aren't you! I love hamsters and baby bunnies. Baby bunnies are my favorite, though.

[Abrupt cut to a new scene]

[Thirty minutes later] Inside Dave's dormitory room:

A basic dormitory room of the 1970s. A "Spartan" environment, furnished with a few pieces of mismatched institutional furniture. The room is basically square, with the door on one side and the windows on the opposite side. There are two single beds that have their long sides pushed against the two remaining walls; and two wooden desks pushed together back-to-back in the center of the room, underneath the windows. Two built-in closets are to the right and left of the entry door and two tall

dressers are pushed against the walls at the foot of each bed. Looking from the entry door, Dave and Laura are seated on the long side of the bed that is pushed against the right wall. The desk closest to them has the deep, bottom drawer open. They sit on the edge of the bed, facing the open drawer. Laura smiles as she snuggles a large, fluffy hamster against her face.

Laura
[baby talk to hamster]
You're a cutey, yes you are. You're a little cutey. **[to Dave]** He's really cute Dave, I can't believe you have him up here.

Dave

We're not supposed to, but anytime someone comes to the door, we just close the drawer so no one ever knows he's here.

[Laura hands the hamster back to him and he puts it gently into the drawer, and then closes it halfway. There's an awkward silence for a few seconds, as they smile at each other]

Laura
[thoughtfully]
You're quite an enigma, Dave. You're very different from most other guys you meet in college today. Good looking, yet kind of shy—that's a rare combination. You're someone with dreams and goals, and you're passionate about the things you love. A rugged hunter and adventurer, yet a sensitive musician who loves Mozart, sailboats, and cuddly little animals. You're the kind of guy that a lot of girls dream about meeting.

[As she says this, she leans toward him and reaches her right hand up to put it on the back of his neck. With her eyelids drooping, she pulls his face downward, opens her mouth, and kisses him deeply and softly. Dave, very excited, puts one hand behind her head and the other on the back of her waist, giving her the kind of kiss that lasts for a very long time. . . . During the lengthy kiss, she slowly reclines back until she is lying on the bed, with her head on the pillow. Dave is now lying on top of her as they continue to kiss. As their lips separate for a moment, she looks into his eyes and whispers something in his ear]

Laura
[softly and romantically]
I feel "bursting!"

Dave
[not quite sure what she said]
What?

Laura
[repeats]
I feel "bursting," like my hearts going to burst!

Dave
[sincerely]
I know what you mean; I kinda feel that way, too.

Laura
[softly]
I think "bursting" is the way I feel when I'm falling in love.

[Still lying on top of her, Dave begins to kiss her again]

[Fade to black]

An upstairs practice room in the music building: Dave sits with Andy in two facing chairs, talking intensely.

Dave

There's no doubt, man; I'm absolutely hooked. I've never felt as strongly about anyone else as I do about Laura right now. I'm head over heels in love with her and I know that I want to marry her!

Andy

[perplexed and frustrated]

Oh that's great! What are you going to tell Kate? "After a year of going together and meeting your parents, I found someone prettier and more exciting than you. But thanks for trusting me enough to let me be the first and only guy you've ever slept with."

Dave

[Jumps to his feet and begins to pace back and forth in front of Andy, pleading his case and trying to convince himself and Andy that he isn't doing a terrible thing]

[feeling guilty] I like Kate, I like her a lot, but she's not very pretty and her looks really don't excite me that much. Shouldn't you spend your life with someone that you are really attracted to physically? Plus, things with Kate are starting to get to be the same old, same old. She's a good friend, probably my best friend next to you, but she's more like one of the guys. We're more like "friends with benefits." We horse around and have fun together, but it's more because she's available and wants to than because I'm in love with her. We're just two kids, lucky enough to have a friend to mess around with until we find the right person.

Laura's like a beautiful fairy-tale princess. The kind of girl a guy dreams about and waits all his life to meet; and she really likes me, too. I'd be the biggest fool in the world to turn my back on a girl like that.

Andy
[standing to leave]
Good luck partner, I'm outta here. Sowing wild oats is one thing, but when you break the heart of a nice girl who trusts you and counts on you without feeling bad it's time for a new wing man.

[Andy leaves the room coldly, and Dave doesn't even try to stop him. He stares at the floor, feeling guilty and looking very sad]

[Abrupt cut to a new scene]

A downstairs practice room in the music building:

Dave and Kate are playing trumpet duets, as they have many times. As they finish a duet Kate smiles broadly, but her expression changes quickly when she turns to see Dave's sad, worried look.

Kate
What's the matter, I know I didn't play that bad.

Dave
Kate, you're a good friend. Actually, you've been the person I enjoy hanging around with the most since we started "going together" last year. You've been like one of the guys and also my "girlfriend," and we've had a lot of fun together. I know that you did things with me for the first time - that are very special and precious to a girl — and I respect and appreciate that very much.

[Pauses a long time]

But I just recently met another girl. I wasn't out looking for someone or planning on it to happen, it just happened. I'm very attracted to her and she's attracted to me, and I'm probably gonna be dating her from now on. I hope you can understand and forgive me, and we can still keep the part of our friendship alive where you're like one of the guys and we get together to play duets and stuff. I really enjoyed coming to your house and meeting your parents and having you meet mine, too. This is very hard for me because you're such a nice girl. Maybe the people who say that first loves and college crushes don't last are right, I dunno.

[He looks across at Kate to see her reaction. She sits in shock, not moving a muscle, looking more crushed and devastated than he has ever seen any human being look. Her eyes are flooded with water, and steady streams of tears pour down the front of her cheeks on both sides. He tries to place his hand on her shoulder to console her, but she thrusts it away violently and screams at him as she runs out of the room and down the hall, banging her fist on the lockers]

Kate [screaming hysterically]
Don't touch me!! What a load of crap!! Loser!! You're nothing but a heartless jerk!! . . . Loser!!

Dave
[Still in the practice room, he lowers his gaze and shakes his head sadly as he hears her heart-broken screams and the pounding of her fist on the lockers fade out as she runs down the hallway]

[Fade to black]

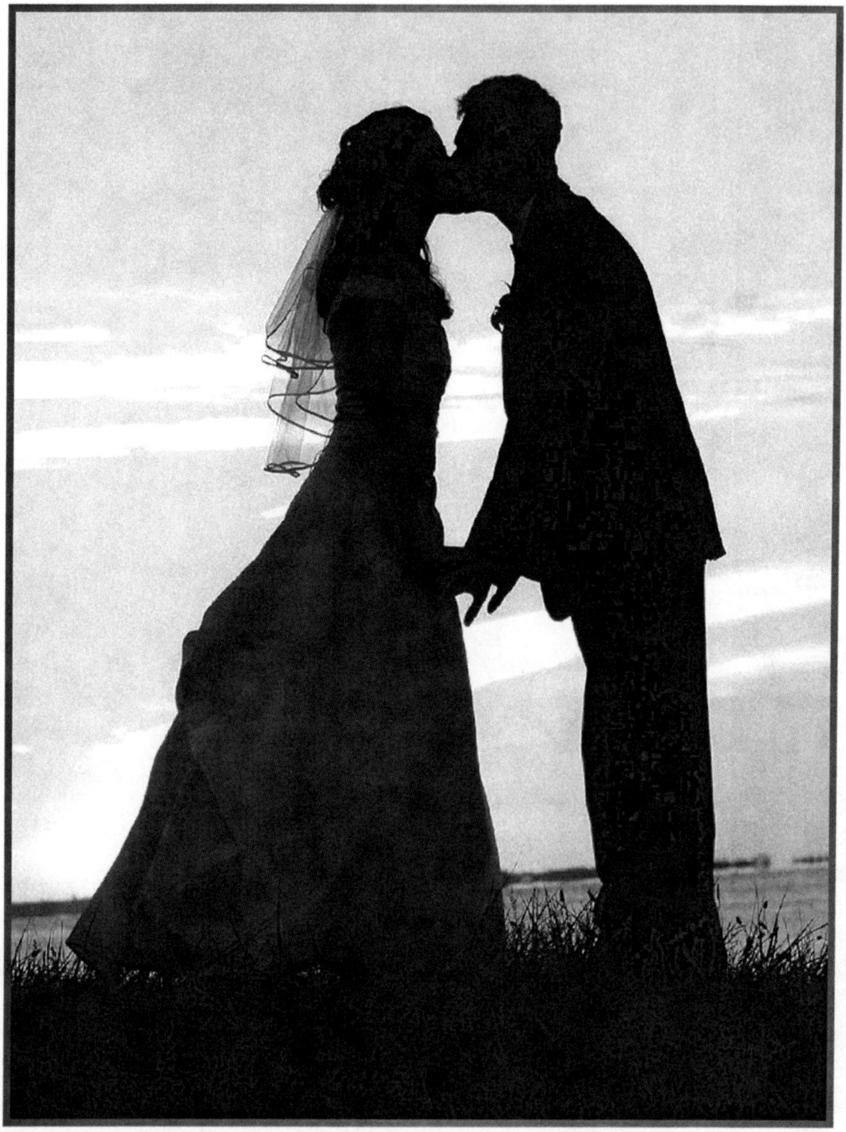

Act 9 •

Married Before My Senior Year Of College

[A series of short vignettes without dialogue, that show Dave and Laura dating, having fun, and spending time together, as their relationship continues and grows throughout the school year]

[Music only]

Vignette #1: Laura and Dave are in a movie theater, smiling and watching a movie together as they share a bag of popcorn and a cold drink. He has his arm around her as the light from the screen flickers on their faces.

Vignette #2: They are sitting at a table in an Italian restaurant, reading menu's as a well-dressed waiter pours wine into their glasses. Laura puts down her menu and smiles. Then she gives the waiter her order and he nods politely as he begins to write it down. [Thirty minutes later] Dave and Laura smile and talk, as they eat from large platters of spaghetti and meatballs.

Vignette #3: They are in a local college bar, slow-dancing in the middle of the dance floor. Laura smiles up at him and they kiss while they are dancing, then she leans her cheek down against his shoulder.

Vignette #4: Dave is meeting Laura's parents and siblings in the living room of her house in Dunkirk. Everyone is smiling and taking turns shaking hands with him as they exchange words of greeting and welcome. Dave, smiling politely, nods and greets each one in turn with a few words as he makes his way around the room.

Laura's mother is a tall, thin, conservatively dressed older woman with short gray hair. Her father is a short, thin, Italian-looking man with a big nose, glasses, and a twinkle in his eye. Her younger sister is taller and more solidly built than Laura; she has short red hair, and is nowhere near as attractive as Laura is. She also has a younger brother who is still in his early high-school years. He is tall for his age and thin with a slight build; and he has thick glasses and buck teeth.

Vignette #5: Laura is meeting Dave's parents, grandparents, and sisters in the kitchen of his parent's home. Everyone's smiling and exchanging handshakes and hugs with her as they greet and welcome her. Laura, smiling politely, greets each one in turn with a hug for the girls and a handshake for the men, as she makes her way around the room.

Dave's grandmother is an invalid with a wooden leg. One of his younger sisters [Jackie] is taller than he is with long dark hair, and his youngest sister [Debbie] is short and petite with curly dark hair.

Vignette #6: Dave and Laura are in a bowling alley. As the scene opens, Dave is in the middle of his delivery and rolls the ball aggressively toward the pins. His ball curves in perfectly for a strike, and Laura applauds excitedly from the scorer's table behind him. He turns to her with a smug smile and flexes his arm muscles, posing like a bodybuilder.

When Laura rolls her ball, she drops it awkwardly, so the ball rolls slowly toward the pins and dribbles off into the gutter just before reaching them. She turns toward Dave, hanging her head and pouting. He motions for her to come back to him, and when she does he gives her a big hug, lifting her petite body completely off the ground and into the air.

Vignette #7: It's Thanksgiving Day at Laura's house and Dave is there having Thanksgiving dinner. Everyone is seated around the bountifully filled dining room table as Mrs. Malone carries a huge golden brown turkey in from the kitchen. There is applause and cheering as she places it on the table, and Mr. Malone starts to carve it.

Vignette #8: It's Christmas at Dave's house and everyone is in the living room, seated around a beautifully decorated tree. New clothing and other gifts that have already been unwrapped lay in piles around the room and there are also many beautifully wrapped gifts still under the tree. Everyone is smiling, laughing, and talking at once. Laura, sitting cross-legged on the carpet, opens a beautiful sweater, and with her mouth and eyes wide open holds it up in front of her while she thanks Dave's mom and dad and gives them a big thumbs up.

Vignette #9: It's a beautiful spring day and Dave and Laura are in a sailboat out on the lake. Dave is pointing and giving Laura instruction. She sits in the stern steering the small craft smiling proudly while Dave works the ropes and the sails. The scene ends with a close-up of the tiny boat with it's billowed sails gliding picturesquely along toward the setting sun.

[**Abrupt cut to a new scene**]

[**A few days later**] Dave and Laura are riding in Dave's car:

Dave

I'm glad we could spend the last few days of spring break at my house. Did you like sailing the boat?

Laura

It was amazing to feel it move that fast with just the wind!

Dave

Maybe someday when we're rich, famous, and married we'll have one big enough to live in, and we can sail it to Florida and the Bahamas. The big ones are just like an apartment inside, you know.

Laura

[stuck up, "southern belle" attitude]

Mr. Tripiciano, is that your lame, roundabout way of proposing to me? I'll have you know that I've had lots of boyfriends, but none of them ever mentioned marriage before. What makes you think I'd marry a man like you anyway? Some good-looking, fly by night, dreamer; who sails boats and plays music! Just what kind of a girl do you think I am sir?! **[Laughs]**

Dave

[dead serious]

The kind of girl that I would marry tomorrow, if she let me.

Laura

[excited]

How about next spring, a year from now, right after I graduate? That would give us time to plan. (There's a lot to plan you know.) It can be a June wedding. (How romantic!) I can't wait to tell mom and Jan, they're gonna be so excited!

Dave

So I take that as a yes then?

Laura

[smiling]

Yes, yes, yes! What did you think I'd say? "Get lost, loser?"

Dave

It's gonna be really hard to be apart over summer vacation.

Laura

We don't have to be. Now that you're my fiancé, mom will let you live at our house over the summer — we've got a spare room.

Dave

But I've gotta get a summer job to keep paying for college.

Laura

Kraft foods in Dunkirk, hires lots of extra summer help!

Dave

That could work! My mom and dad would go for that, if I had a job.

[Abrupt cut to a new scene]

Another series of short vignettes without dialogue that shows Dave working and living at Laura's house through the summer. [There is music only (no dialogue)]

Vignette #1: Dave is working in a food processing plant. Wearing a head net and an industrial uniform with the words "Kraft Foods" on it, he stands at a conveyor belt as cases of barbecue sauce move past him. He and an African-American man are grabbing the cases off of the conveyor and stacking them quickly onto a pallet.

Vignette #2: Dave slowly pulls his car into the driveway of Laura's parent's home at the end of a workday, still wearing his Kraft foods uniform and head net. He looks dead tired as he puts the car in park and turns it off. With great effort he pushes the door open and rises from the car, but from the way he walks and moves it's pretty clear that he has lots of aches and pains. Laura comes bounding out of the door to greet her "hero", who forces a smile as they embrace.

Vignette #3: Dave and Laura are in church on a Sunday morning, along with her parents and younger brother. As the congregation rises to sing a hymn, they rise and open the hymn book they are sharing. As they begin to sing, Laura elbows Dave playfully and gives him a smile.

[More vignettes to show them during Laura's senior year, as they plan for her graduation and the wedding. Music only (no dialogue)]

Vignette #4: Dave is performing in a band concert on the stage of the college's brand-new, state-of-the-art concert hall and performing arts center. The conductor and all of the band members are dressed in formal tuxedoes and black gowns, making the impressive-sounding group also look very professional. Dave plays an important trumpet solo in one of the band pieces, and Laura smiles and applauds proudly when she hears it.

Vignette #5: A wedding dress shop in March: Dave, Laura's mom, and her sister, Jan, wait eagerly in a large room surrounded by mirrors while Laura tries on a wedding gown in one of the fitting rooms. As she emerges into the large room wearing it, Dave rises with his mouth open, stunned by how beautiful she looks. Her mother and Jan nod eagerly with broad smiles, and begin applauding and showering her with thumbs ups and compliments as they fuss with her dress.

Vignette #6: Laura's college graduation. A large class of graduates dressed in caps and gowns is seated on the stage of the college performing arts center. As a group of them in a single line file down from their seats to the front of the stage, Laura is seen, smiling happily in her cap and gown. She stops at the podium to wait for the person ahead of her to walk across the stage, shake hands, and receive a degree; then she walks proudly across the stage to receive hers, as Dave and her parents cheer, applaud, and snap pictures.

[Abrupt cut to a new scene]

[One month later] Dave's parent's home in Auburn, during spring break: Dave is standing in the kitchen, holding a document and a pen in his right hand as he talks to his mother and father.

Dave's Mother
Are you sure you want to do this, David? Twenty years old is awfully young to be making a commitment for the rest of your life.

Dave
I love her, mom. I'm more sure about this than anything else I've ever done. You guys have to sign this form saying that you give me permission to get married, because I'm not twenty-one yet.

Dave's Mother

Okay. . . . Well, she does seem like a nice girl — give me that.

[He hands the document and pen to his mother, who signs it on the table while his dad looks over her shoulder. When she finishes, she hands the pen to his father, who signs his name below hers]

[Abrupt cut to a new scene]

Dave and Laura's wedding in Dunkirk, New York:

Dave's in his tuxedo and Laura's in her wedding gown; they stand facing each other before her pastor at the front of the church, as their friends and families look on. The maid of honor is Laura's sister, Jan, and the groomsmen are Dave's buddies from the music department. As the couple begins to say their vows, Dave's mother sobs loudly into a tissue.

Dave

[smiling at Laura]

I, David, take you, Laura, to be my lawfully wedded wife, my constant friend, my faithful partner, and my love from this day forward. In the presence of God and our family and friends, I offer you my solemn vow to be your faithful partner in sickness and in health, in good times and in bad, and in joy as well as in sorrow. I promise to love you unconditionally, to support you in your goals, to honor and respect you, to laugh with you and cry with you, and to cherish you for as long as we both shall live.

Laura

[smiling at Dave]

I, Laura, take you, David, to be my lawfully wedded husband, my constant friend, my faithful partner, and my love from this day forward. In the presence of God and our family and friends, I offer you my solemn vow to be your faithful partner in sickness and in health, in good times and in bad, and in joy as well as in sorrow. I promise to love you unconditionally, to support you in your goals, to honor and respect you, to laugh with you and cry with you, and to cherish you for as long as we both shall live.

Pastor

By the authority vested in me by Almighty God and the state of New York, I now pronounce you man and wife. You may kiss your bride.

[Dave and Laura kiss softly and tenderly and then turn to walk down the aisle to loud traditional organ music; they are followed by all of their bridesmaids and groomsmen. They are showered with rice and confetti on the steps of the church as they exchange hugs with their teary-eyed mothers and sisters and handshakes with their dads and other family members and friends.

[A few moments later Dave and Laura are waving happily as they pull away in a car lettered, "*Just Married*"]

[Fade to black]

[Another series of short vignettes without dialogue to show Dave and Laura establishing a life together] They find an apartment, adopt a dog, and Laura accepts her first teaching position. Then Dave heads back for his senior year of college.

[Background music only, throughout]

Vignette #1: Dave and Laura are following a short, heavy-set, dark-haired man up a sidewalk toward the side porch of an older

duplex home. As they climb the porch steps, they see a large sign that says, "*Apartment For Rent*". The man opens the door and motions for them to go in. Once inside, the man shows them the living room and then the kitchen. He motions around each room, pointing out and explaining things as Laura and Dave nod with approval and look at each other with excited smiles. As they step back onto the porch, Dave and Laura eagerly shake hands with him. As they go back down the steps, the man takes the sign down and takes it with him.

Vignette #2: An animal shelter. Dave and Laura are in a concrete building lined with cages. Homeless dogs and puppies bark and peer out from cages on both sides of them as they walk slowly down a center aisle. They stop with tender-hearted smiles at a cage containing a cute, half-grown but undernourished beagle puppy. As they put their fingers through the fencing the puppy wags its tail and its whole body as it licks their fingers eagerly. [A few minutes later] Dave drives, while Laura sits on the passenger side holding the puppy on her lap, giggling as it licks her face.

Vignette #3: Laura's in a bright, clean, modern elementary school, where she's being interviewed for a position as a teacher. She is dressed in a suit and skirt, and she smiles and nods eagerly as she is interviewed by a professional-looking, well-dressed woman with glasses. The woman seems to like Laura and smiles as she proudly gives her a tour of the classrooms and facilities in her building. The interview ends with the woman handing Laura a folder and some books and shaking her hand vigorously with both hands. It's clear that she got the job.

Vignette #4: Dave is seated at the kitchen table of their apartment. The table is set for dinner as Laura, smiling proudly, brings a large plate of spaghetti and meatballs to the table and sets it in front of her husband. Dave smiles up at her, nodding with approval; then he gives her a quick kiss on the lips.

[Later] They are getting in bed for the night. They are under the covers with bare shoulders and their heads are on their pillows as they face each other, smiling. As they move toward each other to kiss, Dave flips off the light.

Vignette #5: Dave and Laura are taking their beagle for a walk down a residential street near their apartment. They hold hands and smile as Laura holds the dog's leash; laughing, they run to catch up with the dog as he chases after squirrels and birds along the way.

Vignette #6: Laura is at school, in her classroom, on her first day as a teacher. She stands erect with her shoulders back and a big smile, as she points to the blackboard. She is pointing to her name, which she has written on the board in big letters, and is moving her mouth slowly with large, exaggerated movements, as she pronounces it for the children. She speaks loudly:

Laura
[comically, with large mouth movements]
Mrs. Tri – pi – cia – no.

Class of Second Graders [Answer together]
Mrs. Tri – pi – cia – no.

[Abrupt cut to a new scene]

Act 10 •

Womanizing As A Club Musician - And A Divorce

[Early December 1972] In a practice room in the music building:

Dave is playing a complex classical trumpet solo. At the piano accompanying him is a very attractive blonde girl with long straight hair and glasses. The girl is an accomplished pianist and the interplay between the trumpet and piano are perfect.

Dave
[as they stop playing]
Wow! You are quite the piano player, Beth! Fast fingers, very musical, and a great follower! Looks like the piano department sent me the perfect person to accompany me for my senior recital.

Beth
[imitating Elvis]
Thank you, thank you very much, I'll be here all week. [Laughs]

Dave
[flirting shamelessly]
It's hard not to notice that you're also very beautiful.

Beth
[suddenly curt, professional]
Thank you, I enjoy accompanying you, you're a great player.

Dave

[coming on to her]

I bet you and I could make beautiful music together outside of the music building too, (if you know what I mean).

[He moves in behind her as he says this and puts his hand lightly on her shoulder. As he does, she tenses and her eyes widen]

Would you ever consider messing around with a married guy just for the fun of it?

[She jerks her shoulder away sharply and gathers her music off the piano as she rises to leave]

Beth

[with a no-nonsense tone]

You just answered your own question. You're married; therefore, I would never consider it. Nor would I ever have any interest in a guy who is married and still capable of asking a girl that. I'm required to accompany you by my piano professor and you can rest assured that I will do an excellent job. But please keep this a "working" relationship and limit your comments to the music.

Dave

[laughs nervously]

I'm married, not buried, and it never hurts to have a little fun on the side, if you're discreet. Besides, girls are allowed to sow a few wild oats too these days; it's the seventies, remember?

Beth

[curtly]

Please stop, or I'll ask to be assigned to another soloist. I'm losing more respect for you with every word you say. Call me if, and when, you are ready to seriously rehearse for the recital.

[Abrupt cut to a new scene]

[Early January 1973]
In a practice room, somewhere in the music building:

Dave is alone in the room, standing up as he plays his trumpet. He is practicing scales and exercises when a thin, dark-haired saxophone player enters the room. The young man has thick, heavy, Buddy Holly-style glasses on and is carrying an alto saxophone that is hooked onto the neck strap around his neck. He speaks:

Sax Player
Sounds good dude, sounds good. Hey, sorry to barge in on you like this man, but I might have a really neat job opportunity for you. I've been playing with this band in Dunkirk, but I'm gonna be student teaching out of town this semester, so I can't do it anymore. I promised the guy I'd try to find him someone else here at the college, and he said he'd really like to have a good trumpet player. The good news is: they play every weekend, the music's easy, and you make a lot of money. The bad news is: it's a polka band and they play the same polkas, polish music, and corny old songs over and over.

Dave
That wouldn't bother me a bit after working at Kraft Foods for one whole summer! I'm married and we could really use the money, too. Playing the trumpet for a few hours each week would be the best part-time job ever! Good money, with a minimum of time spent, and I'd be getting paid for something I'm good at, and fun to do!

Sax Player
Here's his number—give him a call. It's a guy and his brother that have the band. A couple of very nice, down-to-earth Polish guys,

that love having a band and playing music. They're actually farmers who live up in the hills, and they're easily impressed. They'll probably think you're the world's greatest trumpet player.

[Smiles, hands Dave the number, and walks out of the room]

Dave
[calls after him]
Hey, thanks man, thanks a lot! **[Then looks at the number]**

[Abrupt cut to a new scene]

[Four weeks later] Saturday night at the Dunkirk VFW Club:

A large, dimly lit rectangular room with a low ceiling that looks like it could have been a basement at one time. There is a semi-circular bar on one end of the room, starting and ending at the wall, and the remainder of the room is a small dance floor with a bandstand in the corner farthest from the entry door. The club looks like it has seen better days, and very much like you would expect this type of establishment to look in a small, blue-collar town. There are a few working-class men and women in groups of two and three at the bar and one couple. The band is playing "Please Release Me" and there are two half-drunk older couples slow-dancing. Four musicians stand behind an old-school, dance-band style music stand with the name "Ronnie's Polka Kings" painted on it. The musicians are all wearing matching polka-dot shirts and polyester trousers.

Ronnie, the leader, is in his early thirties with long, sweaty dark hair. He's playing the accordion and crooning the lyrics loudly into a microphone, while his short, chubby, brother, Don, strums along on the guitar. Behind them a large, heavy-set

man sits behind a drum set, precariously balanced on a stool that seems too small to support his weight. Dave is to Ronnie's left, standing next to a tall, lanky, mustachioed bass player who moves and dances while he plays like he's had too many beers. As they finish a song, Ronnie turns to Dave and gives him a thumbs up.

Ronnie
You're doing a great job Dave! This is only your third Saturday night, but you sound like you've been playing with us for years. I'm really glad you called me; you fit in with us real nice.

Dave
Thanks Ron, this is kinda fun, and I really need the money.

Ronnie
Let's take a break and I'll buy you a beer.

Dave
Okay man, sounds good, thanks.

[As the band members sit at a small table near the bar nursing beers, Dave notices a young blonde woman seated at the bar. She keeps turning her head to look and smile at him. Although seated with a couple of older women, she seems quite young and has long blonde hair, bright blue eyes, and a perky smile. He watches as she looks at him then turns to giggle and talk with the women she is with, only to turn and look his way again, smiling like a school girl. He finds her quite attractive and is flattered and amused by her little game]

Dave

[quietly to Ronnie]

Hey Ron, who's that young blonde at the bar that keeps looking over here and smiling at me?

Ronnie

[looks at the bar, then smiles]

Oh, that's Marlene. She's a good kid, cute too, but she's had some tough breaks. She's about the only young person that comes in here regular. Likes to hang out with that older woman she works with 'cause the old dame treats her like a daughter. I guess she's got a kid, too. A cute little redhead named Benny. It's kind of a sad story, I feel sorry for her.

She was sweet on this good-lookin' older guy who used to come in here all the time. He was married, but he was a big flirt and a ladies' man, always bettin' the other guys that he could get her to go for a "ride" with him after last call. One night he got her drunk enough and she did. As soon as he heard she was pregnant, he stopped coming around and dropped her like a hot potato.

Dave

That's too bad, she does look nice; and cute too.

Ronnie

[kidding, pokes Dave]

You better not be looking that way Dave, you're married too. We better get back up there and earn our money. Let's do a set of rock'n roll songs so my man Dave here can sing like a rock star.

[Abrupt cut to a new scene]

[Later that night] The band is on the bandstand performing:

They are playing the classic upbeat rock song "Joy To The World". Dave holds a microphone in one hand and his trumpet in the other as he sings loudly and aggressively, imitating a rock star.

Dave
[singing loudly]
Jeremiah was a bullfrog! He was a good friend of mine! I never understood a single word he said, but I helped him a drinkin' his wine. Yes, he always had some mighty fine wine.

[Continues the song]

As he sings, Marlene stares at him smiling; then she nods as she says something to the older woman she's with. After she talks to her, she looks back at Dave, again smiling broadly and nodding with approval. It's pretty clear that Dave has a fan, and also pretty clear that he's enjoying the attention she's giving him.

Dave
[looking and smiling right at Marlene]
You know I love the ladies . . . love to have my fun, I'm a high night flyer and a rainbow rider, a straight shootin' son of a gun. And I'm a singin', Joy to the world, all the boys and girls now. Joy to the fishes in the deep blue sea; Joy to you and me.

He puts down the microphone and gives her a wink. Then he begins to play the trumpet. The band continues to play an instrumental version of the song.

[Abrupt cut to one hour later]

The band is now playing the classic rock song "Proud Mary" and a few tipsy older couples are trying to "rock out" on the dance floor. As the song ends, Ronnie speaks:

Ronnie
[into the microphone]
We're gonna take another little short break right now, but we'll be back in a while with some of your favorite polkas.

[Abrupt cut to a new scene]

[A few minutes later] Dave is leaning over the bar with his empty glass, trying to get the bar tender's attention to order a beer. He has deliberately "bellied up" to the bar in the open spot next to Marlene. She sits on a bar stool just a couple of feet away from him. She smiles at him warmly and speaks:

Marlene
[smiling eagerly]
Looks like the new guy playin' with Ronnie is adding a lot to the group. That was some pretty good singin' and trumpet playin' up there. Where you from new guy?

Dave
I'm studying music at the college, so this kind of music's easy for me. I'm hoping to become a school band director some day.

Marlene
If the band director at my high school looked like you, I would have learned to play an instrument and joined the band right away.

Dave
[approaches her with his drink]
You're not so bad lookin' yourself. It's hard not to notice that when you're the youngest and best lookin' girl in the place.

She is flattered and smiles like a schoolgirl when he says this. He is now leaning on the bar right next to her, talking to her.

Dave
[offers his hand for a handshake]
Dave, Dave Tripiciano. (That's Italian).

Marlene
[shakes his hand smiling]
Marlene, Marlene Skalicky. (Polish, very Polish).

Dave
Ronnie says you have a really cute little boy; I love kids.

Marlene
[Smiling proudly, she takes a photo out of her wallet]
A redhead, cutest little guy ever. Can you tell he's Polish?

Dave
[Laughs]
Wow, he is cute! (And Polish!) Look at that big head!

Marlene
He's a little scamp! Three years old, goin' on twenty-three.

Dave
[looking toward the bandstand]

Uh oh, Ronnie's heading back up, so I guess I better get up there. Hey, if you wanna hang around till we're done packin' up, I'll give you a ride home, and maybe we can talk some more?

Marlene

[hesitates, then gives in]

Sure, why not? You're good-lookin' and you seem nice; and I've never been offered a ride home from a guy who plays in a band.

[Abrupt cut to a new scene]

[Ninety minutes later] The front seat of Dave's car. Dave is driving and Marlene sits on the passenger side. He's talking:

Dave

I thought we'd take a ride for a while to get to know each other a little bit before I take you home, is that okay?

Marlene

I don't care, I feel safe with you and I got nothin' to do when I get home except sleep anyway. Besides, I've never had the chance to hang out with a guy like you before.

Dave

What do you mean, "a guy like me?"

Marlene

You know, a college guy: smart, talented, good-looking, nice, wants to be a teacher, plays in a band, knows that I've got a kid and still wants to give me a ride home. . . .

Dave

[turning the car and then slowing]

There's a little dirt road here that goes back through the field and runs along the railroad tracks. I go rabbit hunting here all the time with my beagle. Let's park here and talk awhile. No one will see us back here in the dark. **[Shuts off the car]**

Dave

[honestly]

I've got a confession to make: I'm very attracted to you. Not just your looks either, but your whole personality and attitude are very appealing to me . . . [**pauses]** but I'm a married man.

Marlene

[used to disappointment]

Just my luck! It figures, the good guys always are. Well, if you're parking here hoping we can mess around, I just can't. The last time I messed around with a married guy I wound up alone with a kid, and I promised myself I'd never do that again.

Dave

I know, Ronnie told me about it and I felt bad for you. That's why I wanted to be honest with you right up front.

Marlene

Well, if you want to neck for a while we can do that, but that's as far as I can go. At least then I can tell my sisters that I got to make out with a really cute college guy that plays in a band.

She slides over next to Dave and turns her face to him. Putting his arms around her he begins to kiss her softly with an open mouth. She moves her head back and forth during the kiss and

presses into him, putting one hand behind his head and the other behind his shoulder.

[Fade to black]

[Forty minutes later] The front seat of Dave's car. Dave is smiling as he drives, and Marlene is sitting next to him.

Dave
That was nice, very nice. You're a good kisser!

Marlene [laughs]
You really are an odd one, and a very different kinda guy, if you had that much fun just kissing and not getting anything.

Dave
There's something special and different about you that I really like. You're so much more real and down to earth than my wife; she's kind of uppity with her haiku poetry. I really liked hanging out with you and spending time with you tonight.

Maybe we can be friends, really good friends, and I can hang out with you on Saturday nights when I play in the band? If I can sneak away now and then maybe I can even do some fun stuff with you and your little boy, and help you take care of him. That'd be pretty cool.

Marlene
Oh yeah, sure! I'm already getting the "maybe we can just be friends" line. Believe me, I know how this works. Married guy, plus single girl with a kid; - plus, takes her parking and doesn't get anything, equals: she'll never see or hear from him again.

Dave [laughs]
No, you're wrong, you'll see. I have your number and I'll call you tomorrow. Wait and see.

Marlene
I'll believe it when I see it. That's my house up there on the left, the gray one. Benny and I live with my parents. Thanks for wanting to give me a ride home.

Dave
[as he stops the car]
Thanks for letting me . . . and for a great time.

Marlene
[looks at him bewildered]
You really are very different . . . mmmmmmm . . .

She doesn't get to finish this sentence as Dave kisses her goodnight very deeply and passionately, and she makes no attempt to pull away.

[Fade to black]

The next day, mid-afternoon, in the bedroom of Dave's apartment.
Dave is on the phone, kind of hiding out in the far corner of the room. He speaks quietly as he faces into the corner, looking nervous. On the other end of the line Marlene picks up the phone at her house.

Marlene
[speaking into phone]
Hello?

Dave

How ya doin', blonde Polish girl? I told you I'd call you.

Marlene

[smiles, pleasantly surprised]

You know you really are crazy, even for a musician.

Dave

Crazy about you, blondie; how's little Benny?

Marlene

[smiles warmly]

He's eating lunch and getting more on his face and clothes than in his mouth, the little scamp. Your wife is gonna shoot you, if she catches you talking to some blonde single mother from a bar.

Dave

She's in the shower right now, so I thought I'd give you a quick call. She'll never know I was on the phone. We're playing at the Vet's Club again this Saturday. Hope to see you there.

Marlene

[teasing]

I might be, if the mood strikes me. I heard the band's pretty good.

[Abrupt cut to a new scene]

[Another series of short vignettes that show Dave spending time with Marlene on Saturday nights when he plays in the band.

A couple of the scenes also show him spending time with her and her son during the day, while Laura is teaching or when he is otherwise able to get away.]

[Background music only; unless otherwise noted]

Vignette: #1 The band is playing energetically at the VFW as couples whirl and dance the polka. Among the crowd is Marlene dancing with her older female companion. She dances this traditional Polish dance like an expert who really knows her stuff. Having a great time, she flashes Dave a smile. He gives her a wink and a thumbs up with one hand as he continues to play the trumpet with the other.

Vignette: #2 Marlene is seated at the bar sipping a beer and Dave is standing at the bar next to her. They laugh and smile as they sip their drinks, lean into each other, and elbow each other playfully.

Vignette: #3 They are in the front seat of Dave's car — parked in the same spot as the night they met — kissing very passionately.

Vignette: #4 Dave's house on a Saturday afternoon. Dave is grabbing hunting clothes, boots, and a shotgun out of a closet. Then carrying his "gear," he walks into the kitchen where Laura is stirring a pot.

Dave
Bye babe, I'm goin' rabbit huntin' with the dog down by the tracks. I should be back soon after it gets dark.

[She turns her head and they exchange a quick peck on the lips]

Laura [calling after him]
Have fun, but try not to let the dog get burdocks all over her.

Vignette #5: An interior shot of Dave's car. There we see Dave's hunting clothes, hat, boots, and shotgun on the back seat of the empty car, as if forgotten. The car is parked on a dirt access road that runs along a set of railroad tracks. Outside the car, Dave and Marlene are kneeling on the ground on both sides of her son, encouraging him to pet Dave's beagle. Dave holds the dog's collar as he gently puts the three-year-old's hand on the dog's head; then both adults laugh as the dog licks the boy's face.

Vignette #6: The band is playing at the VFW club again, and the floor is filled with people happily dancing the polka. Dave plays the trumpet, as Marlene polkas past him, dancing with a female friend. Dave puts his trumpet down and walks out on the dance floor. - Tapping Marlene's partner on the shoulder, he says something in her ear. The woman smiles, nods, let's go of her, and backs away. Dave grabs Marlene and polkas her all around the floor; she smiles and the other dancers applaud, as Ronnie and the band members look at each other laughing and shaking their heads.

[Abrupt cut to a new scene]

[A few days later] An older gray-haired woman is standing in her kitchen, talking on the telephone. On the other end of the line is Laura's mother.

Older Woman
Pauline? Pauline Malone? This is Jean, Jean Simmons from church. I hate to be the one to tell you this Pauline, but your daughter Laura's husband is cheating on her!

Mrs. Malone
[shocked]
What! You've got to be kidding me! That can't be possible, they haven't even been married a year yet!

Older Woman
[gossiping]
No, I'm sorry to say it, but it's absolutely true. Jenny's husband is a World War II vet and he loves Polish music. He takes her down to the VFW on Saturday nights to hear the band. Your son-in-law does play the trumpet in a polka band, doesn't he?

Mrs. Malone
[devastated]
Yes, he does it for extra money, but I can't believe what you're telling me. Laura will be crushed, absolutely crushed!

Older Woman
Jenny recognized him from church. Apparently, he's been openly having an affair with this young woman for quite some time. She's some working-class, blonde Polish girl with an illegitimate child, who hangs out at the bar of the vet's club on Saturday nights.

Mrs. Malone
[getting madder]
Just like a musician. That dirty little Italian rat!

Older Woman
They say that it's shameful the way they carry on. They laugh, drink, and even dance together; and she usually leaves the club with him at the end of the night when the band is done playing.

Mrs. Malone
[furious]
That sneaky little Italian liar! I can't believe he would do this to her! Thanks for the call Jean; I'll handle this.

[Abrupt cut to a new scene]

[A Saturday afternoon] The street where Dave and Laura live:

As Dave's car comes down the street, it's apparent that he's coming home from "hunting". He has his hunting hat on, and his shotgun is on the back seat. His hunting coat is thrown on the front seat where the dog is happily sitting on it with her tongue hanging out as she looks out the window. As he pulls into a parking space in front of his apartment, he sees Laura's parent's car pulled up on the grass next to the porch. The trunk and both back doors of the car are open, and it's filled with cardboard boxes and Laura's suitcases.

Leaving the dog and his gear behind, he gets quickly out of the car and looks into the other vehicle. A shocked expression comes to his face as he sees that most of Laura's clothes and personal belongings have been loaded into it. Moving toward the porch, he calls out loudly:

Dave
[loudly, desperately]
Laura . . . Laura, what's going on!

There is no answer to his loud cries, but as he reaches the porch the front door bursts open and out come Mr. and Mrs. Malone followed by Laura, each carrying large boxes and clothes on hangers to the car. Her parent's faces are filled with hate and Laura's eyes are filled with tears as they push past him roughly, disregarding his questions and his presence completely. Dave grabs Laura's arm to stop her and tries to ask her what is going on, but she jerks it away angrily and screams at him through her tears.

Dave [yelling frantically]
Laura! What's happening! Where are you goin' with all your stuff?

Laura [jerks away then screams]
Don't touch me!! Don't you ever touch me again!! How could you? How could you possibly . . . We haven't even been married a year!! I'm leaving, you cheating liar!! You horrible, cheating, liar!!

Mrs. Malone
[angry and vicious]
Laura has already spoken to our lawyer about getting an annulment. Since you weren't married a year, she should be granted one with no problem. You'll be receiving the papers in the mail soon.

Laura and her parents get into the car, slam the doors shut, and drive away. Dave stands there staring sadly after them, looking very guilty and feeling very much alone.

[Abrupt cut to a new scene]

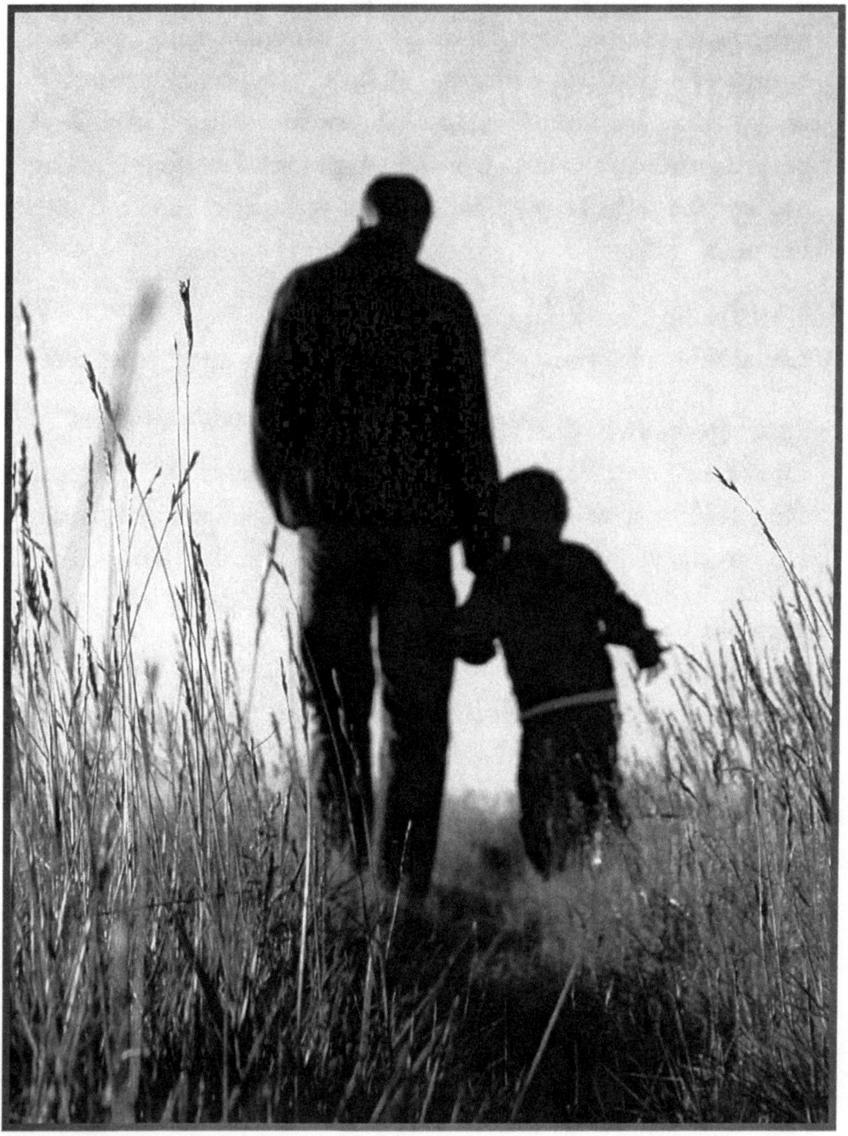

Act 11

Married Again With A Little Boy Who Loved Me

[One year later] The altar of a Catholic Church in Dunkirk:

Dave's in a tuxedo standing next to Marlene in a wedding gown. They stand before a priest on the altar of the Catholic Church. Slightly behind and between them is Benny, also in a tux and holding the small white pillow of a ring bearer. The little redhead smiles broadly as he looks up at the two of them. He is holding the hand of a dark-haired flower girl who is wearing a bridesmaid's dress and holding a basket. As the priest prays, the small congregation joins in: Dave's parents and just a few of his relatives on one side, and Marlene's parents and a much larger turn-out on her side of the church.

Catholic Priest
Please turn to face each other now to recite your wedding vows.

Dave
[smiling at Marlene]
I David, take you, Marlene, to be my wedded wife. To have and to hold, from this day forward, for better or for worse, for richer or for poorer, in sickness and in health, to love and to cherish, till death do us part. And hereto, I pledge you my faithfulness.

Marlene
[smiling at Dave]
I Marlene, take you, David, to be my wedded husband. To have and to hold, from this day forward, for better or for worse, for richer or for poorer, in sickness and in health, to love and to cherish, till death do us part. And hereto, I pledge you my faithfulness.

Catholic Priest
I now pronounce you man and wife. You may kiss your bride.

The organ starts to play loudly as Dave and Marlene share a long tender kiss. Then they turn to walk down the aisle, with Benny between them holding both of their hands. As they step outdoors smiling, they are showered with rice and confetti. Then they begin to exchange hugs and handshakes with their family and friends. As the hugs and handshakes end and the crowd disperses, Marlene is involved in a conversation with her parents. Seeing her chance to talk to him privately, Dave's mother pulls him aside for a few moments, to ask him some questions and express some concerns.

Dave's Mother
[quietly]
Congratulations honey, she does seem like a nice girl and her little boy has to be the cutest little guy I've ever seen. **[pauses]** I can almost accept the fact that the first one didn't work out, because in a lot of ways (at least in my mind) you weren't really married:
#1 You were way too young to be getting married (and I knew it).
#2 You didn't get married in a Catholic Church.
#3 It didn't even last a year, and . . .
#4 It was annulled, meaning the marriage was never really valid.

But! **[long pause]** You better make sure you make this one work! There's a child involved this time, and it looks like he really loves you. Dad and I will be very disappointed if you mess this up, and the rest of the family is going to lose a lot of respect for you too.

[she continues] Where are you guys going to live?

Dave
We bought a new mobile home. A big, state-of-the-art one, that's nicer, and furnished better inside than most brand new houses. It's in a trailer park right now, but Marlene's father gave us an acre of land on his abandoned farm. I'm gonna clear some brush with his old tractor and set it up there. Then we'll have a beautiful home in the country, and lots of room for Benny to play.

Dave's Mother
Sounds nice; how's your new job as a band director?

Dave
Fantastic! Only been there a year, but all the kids seem to like and respect me. I've started a marching band and the principal thinks I'm some kind of hero because the school's never had one.

Dave's Mother
[hugs him]
That's great, honey. I'm happy that things are finally falling into place for you. You be good to her now, and spend lots of time with that little boy. You're the only "father" he's ever had.

[Fade to black]

[Another series of short vignettes without dialogue that show Dave and Marlene's life together over the next year, including: setting up their mobile home in the country, spending time together as a family, working as a marching band director, playing in the polka band, and some very touching scenes of him playing with Benny]

Vignette #1: In a brushy, uninhabited area surrounded by small trees, Dave (covered with dust and dirt) turns the crank on the front of an antique farm tractor to start it. Climbing aboard the chugging, smoke-belching machine he backs it up to three close-together saplings. Climbing down, he wraps a chain around the base of the small trees and hooks it to the back of the tractor, then pulling forward he rips them out of the ground roots and all. Sweating profusely, he drags them over to a large pile of bushes and trees and tosses them onto the pile.

Vignette #2: [Several weeks later] In the same spot; there is now a clearing with a few mature trees left standing. A truck driver is towing a large mobile home through the mud and into the clearing as Dave directs him.

Vignette #3: [A few months later] The mobile home is attractively set up on the property with a metal garage next to it. The dirt clearing has become a spacious green lawn, and there is an above-ground swimming pool in the back yard. A gravel driveway leads from the road to the front of the garage and there are two cars parked side by side in the driveway.

Inside the mobile home is a roomy, attractively furnished, wood-paneled interior. Dave and Marlene sit side by side on the couch, sharing a bowl of popcorn with Benny as they watch TV. The little red head sits happily on Dave's lap with a fistful of popcorn. Smiling, he turns to Dave and shoves one of the kernels into Dave's mouth. Dave rolls his eyes and makes a big deal over this "delicious morsel," as he chews it with slow, exaggerated motions. The child laughs and leans into him.

Vignette #4: Dave is in the middle of a rehearsal with his marching band. The band moves and changes formations on the football field as the students play aggressively, carrying themselves with great pride and precision. He stands at the top of a tall, makeshift tower on the sidelines, yelling directions through an electronic megaphone. He points and makes large, excited gestures, as if he is directing traffic. In a flash, he's out on the field, giving directions to one of the students in the formation face to face. Grabbing the boy's trumpet, he holds it out, demonstrating the perfect playing posture. Then effortlessly picking up his knees very high, he demonstrates marching in place with it while making a slow turn in four counts. He then hands it back to the boy and gives him a pat on the shoulder.

Vignette #5: Dave and Marlene walk along a gravel beach somewhere on Lake Erie, near Dunkirk. Benny (older now) is with them and Dave is holding his hand as they walk. They stop and Dave shows him how to throw a stone in the water. The little boy smiles, then picks up a stone from the beach and tries to throw it into the water but it lands short. Moving down to the water's edge he tries again and this time his stone lands in the lake, resulting in much applause and cheering from Marlene and Dave. Dave then lifts him high and places him on his shoulders for a ride.

Vignette #6: Christmas at Dave's parent's house. Dave, Marlene, Benny, Dave's parents, his grandparents, and his sisters all sit around the living room with warm smiles as they open gifts, laugh, talk, and bask in the glow of a beautifully decorated tree. Dave's father gives him a nod and the two of them quietly leave the room. They return a moment later carrying a complete drum set that's just the right size for a little boy. Benny's eyes widen in amazement and he jumps up and down ecstatically when he sees it. Putting it down and arranging the pieces, Dave hands the boy the drumsticks. The little redhead begins to pound wildly on all the drums as everyone laughs.

Vignette #7: Ronnie's "Polka Kings" are playing on the stage of a Polish club in Dunkirk. The walls around the large, well-lit dance floor are decorated with silver streamers and large signs that say: "Happy New Year!" Dave is out on the crowded dance floor in his polka-dot band shirt; he smiles broadly as he expertly dances the polka with Marlene, who seems to be having a great time.

Vignette #8: Dave and Marlene are outdoors in the snow with (a bit older) Benny. The boy is bundled to the max with a snowsuit, scarf, mittens, and leggings, and they're trying to get him to slide down a small hill on a plastic saucer sled. Finally, Marlene sets him into the sled and gives it a shove. Dave, at the bottom of the hill, with open arms catches him. On the way home in the car, Dave is driving and Benny has his snowsuit open and his hood down as he stands on the back seat, leaning over the top of the driver's seat, with his arms around Dave's neck and his head resting on his shoulder.

[Fade to black]

[A year later] The band room of the school, where Dave teaches: **Dave is giving a clarinet lesson to three girls in chairs. He kneels beside the end girl, pointing to her music with a pencil, singing in her ear as she plays. As they finish playing he speaks:**

Dave [encouraging]
Very nice ladies; you've improved a lot since last week, and I'm proud of you. Better pack up now and get back to class.

The girls talk among themselves as they take their clarinets apart and put them away. As they cross the room to leave, there's a knock on the band-room door. Dave, now sitting at his desk working, speaks:

Dave

Who could that be? Girls, can you open the door for whoever that is on your way out and tell them to come in? Thanks guys.

As the girls open the door, a thin woman in her late twenties with short dark hair, a cute face, and wire-rimmed glasses enters. She's carrying an instrument case and a small paper bag in each hand. As the girls exit, she walks into the room smiling brightly.

Joanne
[outgoing, energetic]
Thanks girls, hello Mr. Trip! Delivery from "The Music Center".

Dave
[rises smiling, and approaches her]
Good to see you Joanne. I forgot that you come every Thursday.

Joanne
[joking, teasing flirtatiously, and putting on a fake pout]
Wow, thanks a lot Dave. Here I look forward to seeing the hottest, most up-and-coming young band director in the county every Thursday and he doesn't even remember that I'm coming.

Dave
[laughing]
It won't happen again, Jo. How could I forget about you anyway?

You're so perky and outgoing that I always have fun talking to you at the music store, or when you come to deliver stuff.

Joanne [handing him the instrument cases]
Speaking of deliveries—here's your trumpet, all the dents are gone and it looks as good as new. An alto saxophone with new pads—George said it plays great. **[Hands him the bags]** Five lesson books and an assortment of Rico #3 clarinet, alto, and tenor sax reeds.

Dave [smiling]
Thanks Jo, you made my day. I needed these really bad.

Joanne
[smiling flirtatiously and speaking right into his face]
I shouldn't tell you this, but as I visit the other band directors around the county the word on the street is that this school has gone from no marching band program to an award-winning marching band that no one even wants to be in the same parade with.

Dave
It has become pretty big since I've been here. The kids love it and the parents think it's the greatest thing since sliced bread.

Joanne
[leaning closer, speaking seductively]
You know, *Mr. Tripiciano,* I'm a sucker for gifted, creative men who think outside the box and know how to make things happen. I love winners, strong leaders, and the kind of guys who command respect. But if someone's a mover and a shaker, and also has great looks and a loveable boyish personality, I find him almost impossible to resist.

As she says this, she presses herself against Dave's body and kisses him very seductively on the mouth. Surprised at her aggressiveness, he kisses her back with an open mouth. The kiss lasts several seconds and then she pulls back, looking to see his reaction. He speaks:

Dave
Wow, good kisser. What about your husband, aren't you married?

Joanne
What he doesn't know won't hurt him. Besides he's boring and we never do anything together anymore. I can't even stand to have him touch me — it creeps me out. I think we're going to get a divorce.

Dave
You're very seductive and provocative, and exciting to be around. Maybe I'll call you sometime when I can sneak out of the house.

[Fade to black]

[A week later] The front seat of Dave's car:

It's daylight on a Saturday afternoon. Dave's car is parked in his favorite hunting/parking spot on the dirt road along the tracks. We can't see into the car because the windows are fogged up. Dave is seated in the center of the seat with his body facing the windshield. Joanne is half sitting on his lap and half kneeling on the seat, facing him with her legs straddling him. They are fully clothed, but embracing and kissing passionately as she sits on him with her body pressing against his. As the kiss ends, she gets off his lap and slumps over to sit in the seat next to him, putting her head on his shoulder. She speaks:

Joanne
Doug and I have filed for a divorce, so I'll be single soon.

Dave
That's great, that's what you wanted, isn't it? Marlene's been getting pretty boring and our life just seems to be the same old, same old. We've been arguing an awful lot lately, too. If it wasn't for Benny, I probably would've left months ago; he sure seems to love me a lot. . . . It's really exciting and lots of fun being with you, though. You'd be worth leaving both of them for.

She looks up at him and they begin to kiss again.

[Fade to black]

[Two weeks later] A dumpy room in a cheap motel in Dunkirk:

Dave is alone in the room, seated on the bed talking on the phone. He's having a conversation with Joanne.

Dave
[smiling proudly]
Well, I did it Jo — I left her. She came home from work all grumpy again and started another argument, so I just gathered up my stuff and walked out. Of course, it was a lot easier to leave, knowin' that I had someone new and exciting waiting in the wings. I'm in a cheap motel down by the lake, if you wanna come over.

Joanne
[sadly, coldly]
That's too bad, I hope you didn't leave your wife and that little boy just for me; I don't think I could deal with the guilt from that right now, too. I got word today that my divorce is final.

My emotions are all over the place and I'm having a lot of second thoughts. I've just been released from a seven-year mistake, and I think it would be an even bigger mistake, to jump into another long-term relationship with anyone right now. We had some fun, let's leave it at that. I'll see you in the store. Gotta go, someone's at the door.

She hangs up abruptly, leaving Dave sitting there alone in the dingy, dumpy motel room. He stares blankly at the wall with the phone still in his hand. He's dazed, confused, and crushed. As he hangs up slowly, he shakes his head and looks around the room, making a face as he realizes where he is, that he is alone, and how shabby the room is.

Dave
[Thinking to himself]
Look at this place—what a dump! What am I doing here and what was I thinking?! . . . I've never felt this alone before in my life!

Springing quickly into action he starts to change his clothes and load some study materials into his briefcase. He talks to himself while doing this; then he grabs his coat and exits the room.

Dave [Thinking to himself]
I've gotta get outta here at least for a while. Go some place bright and cheerful, where there are other people around. I've got to get a book at the college library for my graduate class, so I'll hang out there and read, browse, and maybe listen to some music. I'll call Marlene tomorrow and go back home to her and Benny, if she'll take me back.

[Fade to black]

[Minutes later] In the huge, modern, brightly lit college library:

Dave walks between tables of students reading and studying, as he crosses through the study area of the beautiful, state-of-the-art building. He sets his coat and briefcase on a table, and heads down an aisle between bookshelves that seem to go on forever. As he begins to explore and look at book titles, he sees a young woman taking books from a cart, and then placing them carefully on the shelves. The college-age woman is slender, with shoulder-length straight brown hair and a pretty face. Dave approaches her and politely asks her a question:

Dave
[politely]
Excuse me, miss, sorry to bother you, but it looks like you work here. Could you please tell me where the P—Q section is?

The woman turns and gives an expression of being pleasantly surprised as she sees who has approached her. She gives him a bright smile, as though she is greeting an old friend.

Young Woman
[smiling eagerly]
Certainly, I'd be happy to; follow me.

The young woman leads him through the library, being very helpful and very gracious; turning to smile at him as they walk.

Dave

[thinking as they walk]

Why is this cute college girl being so helpful and so nice to me, and why is she smiling at me like she knows me? I feel like I've seen her somewhere before, but I'm not sure; do I know her?

Young Woman

[stops and points, with a smile]

Here we are. The P—Q books start at the end of this bookshelf, and go all the way to the wall. Can I help you find anything else?

Dave

I never forget a face, especially a pretty one. You seem very familiar to me. Did you go to Green Valley High School?

Young Woman

[smiling, respectful]

Yes! And I knew you the moment I saw you, Mr. Tripiciano.

Dave

[all smiles]

That's right; you're the shy, studious girl from the poor family who had lots of brothers and sisters. But you worked very hard to become salutatorian and get a college scholarship. You were a senior my first year there, right? I remember reading about you!

Young Woman

That's right: Cecelia, Cecelia Barber. It's been three years since high school. You've got a good memory, Mr. Tripiciano.

Dave

[laughs]

Like I said, I never forget a face, especially a pretty one. Now please, call me Dave; you're certainly not a schoolgirl any more.

Cecelia

[blushes, giggles]

It feels kind of strange to call one of the teachers by their first name.

Dave

A band director isn't a "real" teacher, and I'm not your teacher now. Besides you weren't even in the band.

Cecelia

No, I wasn't, but all the girls in the band had a crush on you!

Dave

[smiling, flattered]

Oh really, is that so?

Cecelia

Yep, some of my best girlfriends, too.

Dave

I worked hard to make ours the best marching band around.

Cecelia

And you succeeded **[smiles and elbows him playfully]** — DAVE.

Dave

So, Cecelia, you're a junior in college now?

Cecelia

Yes, a math major. The scholarship helped, but coming from a large, poor family, I'm still working my way through. That's why I'm here in the library tonight helping you find the P–Q section.

Dave

You know, I play in a band that has gigs in clubs and bars around town. You'll have to come and listen to us sometime.

Cecelia [flirting]

I'd like that!

Dave

[flirting back]

I'd like that too!

Cecelia

So you already know that I come from a large family with five boys and five girls. How about you, any brothers or sisters?

Dave

I was the only boy with two younger sisters; and I was the hunting and fishing buddy of my dad, so my parents kinda spoiled me.

Cecelia

[flirting]

Well, that would be easy to do.

Dave

[flirting back]

Would you like to spoil me, by having coffee and a dessert with me when you get done with work?

Cecelia

[surprised]

I'm flattered that you'd ask me, but you're married, aren't you?

Dave

[thinking fast]

Actually, and being completely honest with you, I have recently left the home; and my wife and I are currently living apart.

Cecelia

[relieved, smiling]

Well then, I might as well enjoy the company of a handsome, lonely, older man. Besides my girlfriends would be green with envy if they knew I had a "date" with you. I get off at nine o'clock, I'll see you then.

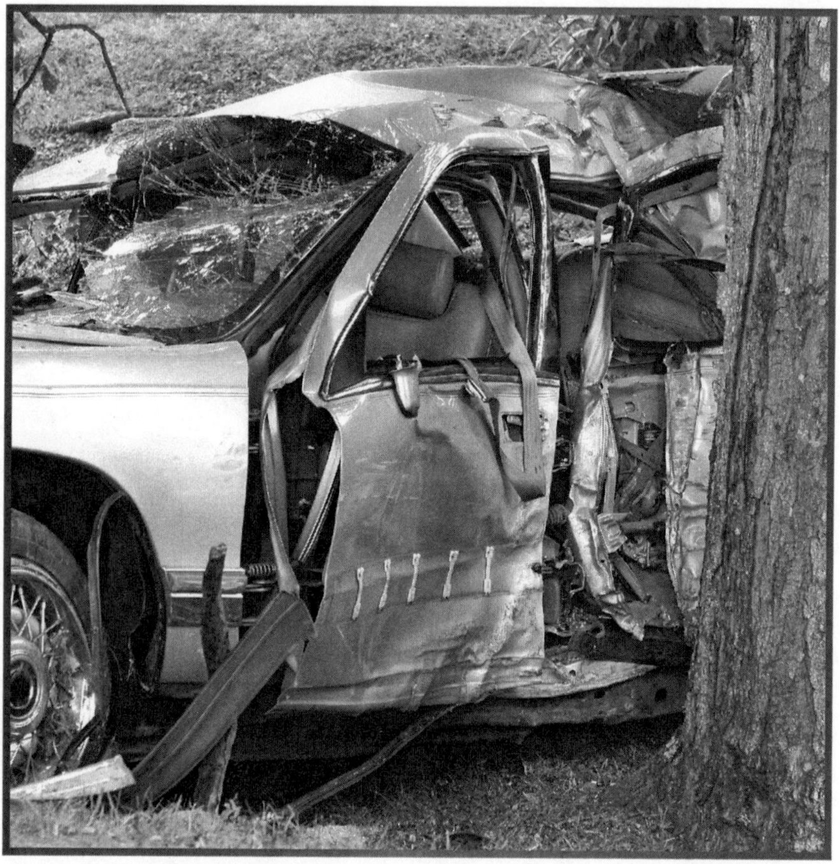

Act 12 •

Nightmare One Morning – A Fatal Car Accident

[A series of three short vignettes without dialogue — musical background only — show Dave and Cecelia having coffee that night, and then a couple more informal "dates" over the next few nights]

Vignette #1: [Later that night] Dave and Cecelia sit at a table in the student center snack bar, having coffee and sharing a piece of chocolate cake à la mode. They laugh, talk, and smile as they eat and sip their coffee. The scene ends with Cecelia placing her hand on Dave's arm and rubbing it, as she smiles warmly.

Vignette #2: Dave and Cecelia are sitting at a table in an Italian restaurant with a red-and-white checkered tablecloth. A waiter brings a large pizza with the works and sets it on the table between them. As Cecelia lifts a piece out of the pie the long, stringy cheese clings and pulls across the table. With one artistic sweep of his hand (like a famous conductor), Dave snags all of the excess cheese; then eats every morsel of it delicately off his fingers, while pretending to be dignified and well mannered. As he does this, Cecelia teases and laughs, shaking her head and her finger at him.

Vignette #3: Dave and Cecelia are in Dave's motel room watching television. They are lying on the bed in a semi-sitting position, with their backs resting against pillows that

are propped against the headboard. They are fully clothed and sitting on top of the covers as they eat from the bowl of popcorn on Dave's lap. Dave has his arm around Cecelia's shoulders as they watch *The African Queen*, with Humphrey Bogart and Katherine Hepburn.

[An hour has passed] The bowl of popcorn is empty, the movie is over, and the credits are rolling down the screen. Dave reaches for the remote and pops off the TV, then he places the empty popcorn bowl on the night stand. Without saying a word or hesitating for a moment, he pulls Cecelia toward him and kisses her very deeply and softly on the mouth. She surrenders to him, moving her head as the two of them continue to embrace and kiss.

[Fade to black]

[The following morning] Outside the door of Dave's motel room:

The door opens and Dave emerges, leading Cecelia by the hand. They are smiling as they walk over to Dave's car and get in.

Dave
Let's get a move on there, missy; I don't want my little math major to be late for her class. Shall I treat you to some coffee?

Cecelia
Yeah, that would be great. My high-school girlfriends would really be green with envy now, if they knew where I was all night. [**Pauses and looks at Dave, smiling**] Last night was beautiful.

Dave
[as he drives]
Yes, it was . . . very beautiful. You've certainly changed any image I had of you being the shy, studious, school girl.

Cecelia
[laughs]

I was shy and studious, but I had a steady boyfriend after high school. Believe it or not he was a big, hefty, bald biker dude. Don't ask me how a girl like me wound up with someone like that. **[sadly she continues]** I guess it happened because he was the first guy who was interested in me that wasn't just one of the nerds from high school. He was an "older guy" and he seemed very nice at first, but he turned out to be crude, demanding, insensitive, and selfish, not tender and thoughtful like you. It was the biggest mistake of my life.

Dave [surprised, encouraging]

Wow, that is a surprise, but I can see how it could happen. Don't feel bad or guilty, that type of thing happens a lot to pretty girls that no one notices in high school. He saw easy "prey" and took advantage of you. Don't let it get you down, you're smart, beautiful, you have a good heart . . . and I think I'm falling in love with you.

Cecelia

[her eyes widen with excitement]

I hate to see you living alone in that dumpy motel room. It's not really the nicest place for us to spend time together either. I share an apartment with three other girls, and I have a bedroom all to myself. You're welcome to share my room with me. The other girls shouldn't care, since one of them has a boyfriend living there with her. The bed's small but at least we'd be together?

Dave

Holy cow! The shy, studious, school girl really is full of surprises today! That's a fantastic offer, ...

[joking, aside in the manner of Groucho Marx] as a matter of fact that's the best offer I've had today.

[She laughs] I'd love to! We'd be together, and if things work out, I can save the money I'm spending on a motel room to someday get us a place of our own!

I've always wanted a place in the country, what do you think? You're a country girl, aren't you? Wouldn't it be nice to have . . . . . **[The scene begins to fade out while he's talking]**

[Fade to black]

[Abrupt cut to a new scene]

[A week later] Dave is talking on the phone to Marlene from a campus phone booth. He has a sad, guilty expression as he talks to her; and Marlene's eyes are filled with tears.

Dave
[sad, and guilty]
I filed for a divorce. The lawyer said it can be quick and easy, or a messy, long, drawn-out process. Please don't make it any harder than it has to be. Just sign the papers and it'll be over.

Marlene
[sobbing; desperately]
Dave, oh Dave! Please, come home, please come back to us! Benny stands at the front window every day with his nose pressed against the glass looking down the road. I keep telling him you're not coming back, but he stands there anyway with a face that breaks my heart, looking like an abandoned puppy. You're the only father he's ever had! My uncle Mike's very sick too, and he might die!

Dave
[wincing with guilt]
I do love Benny very much, but I can't live with the constant fighting and arguing anymore. I need to be with someone who makes me feel loved and looks up to me; and I think I finally found someone like that.

Marlene [getting mad, then yelling]
You're a jerk! You don't even know what real love is, and you'll never understand the kind of love that lasts a lifetime!

Dave
I don't blame you for being hurt and upset, we had a couple of good years and it didn't work out. You guys can have the trailer and stay in it. (It was your father's land anyway). All I want is the piano, because I use it to write music for my marching band.

She slams the phone down angrily and begins sobbing violently. Dave keeps the phone to his ear for a long time as he stares off blankly into the distance. Then he slowly, sadly, hangs it up.

[Fade to black]

[Two weeks later] The bedroom of Cecelia's college apartment:

Dave and Cecelia are lying on Cecelia's small single bed with their backs resting on pillows against the headboard. They are sharing a bag of chips as they watch a tiny TV that rests on top of her cluttered dresser.

Cecelia
What does your wife say about me?

Dave
Oh, it doesn't matter; I've already filed for a divorce. It'll be final in a few weeks.

Cecelia
I'm sorry about the little boy. It sounds like he really loves you.

Dave
[saddens]
He does, and I love him, too. But as hard as it is, if I have to choose between being his dad and being with you—it's no contest.

[She gives him a short but very tender kiss on the mouth]

Cecelia
[shaking her head]
My parents found out that you're living here. **[pause]** They don't like it.

Dave
Really, why?

Cecelia
They're very old-fashioned, and very religious.

Dave
I'm glad you're not.

Cecelia

But I respect them and their faith, so I go to church with them. Why don't you go with us? They'd like that and think more of you.

Dave

Sure, why not.

[Abrupt cut to a new scene]

[A short vignette of Dave going to church with Cecelia and her parents. During this scene there is no dialogue or musical background. Instead, we hear Dave speaking as a narrator, sharing his feelings and explaining what is happening as the scene unfolds]

Dave

[narrating the scene below]

I really didn't care how Cecelia's parents felt about us living together, but going to church with them painted me with respectability and helped me to win points with them and with her, so I went. . . .

Dave and Cecelia climb the steps of a small, average-looking church. Inside the front door a very humble looking older couple greets them with sincere smiles. The sweet, gentle couple has several children with them. They and their children are very poorly and shabbily dressed. After exchanging handshakes and hugs, they all move up the center aisle to find a seat. The group takes up an entire pew halfway toward the front on the left side. They all rise to sing, as the service begins.

[Abrupt cut to a new scene]

[Later, in the same church service; the action now has live dialogue]:

The pastor, an older gray-haired man, gives the sermon from the pulpit.

Pastor

. . . but Matthew 5:28 says: "It has been said in my commandments; do not commit adultery, but I tell you that anyone who looks at a woman lustfully, has already committed adultery with her in his heart."

[Dave looks convicted and very guilty as he hears this verse]

Pastor

. . . and Matthew 5:32 says: "Anyone who divorces his wife, except for marital unfaithfulness, causes her to become an adulteress, and any man who then marries the divorced woman commits adultery himself."

[Dave slides down in his seat, feeling further conviction and guilt as he hears this verse]

. . . then in John 4:18 we read: "Jesus said to her, you are right when you say you have no husband. The fact is that you have had five husbands and the man you are living with now is not your husband."

[Dave and Cecelia look at each other wide-eyed as they hear this]

[Abrupt cut to a new scene]

[Thirty minutes later] At the back of the church; the service has just ended:

People smile and exchange handshakes with each other and the pastor as they linger for a few minutes after the service. Dave is standing next to Cecelia's mother, a humble woman with a very sweet and gentle spirit.

Mrs. Barber
[to Dave, smiling sincerely]
Cecelia said you're in the process of a divorce?

Dave
[embarrassed]
Yes, I've made some mistakes, but I've learned from them.

Mrs. Barber
[sincerely warm and caring]
Then today's sermon must've been very difficult for you to hear.

Dave
[squirming nervously, but being honest]
I hate to admit it, but it was scary! It was almost like the pastor knew I would be here and he wrote the sermon just for me.

Mrs. Barber
[smiling warmly]
Well the pastor didn't know you'd be here, but I can guarantee that someone else did; and I'm sure he gave the pastor just the words that you needed to hear today. Don't worry about the mistakes and sins of the past. When you accept Jesus they are washed away, forgiven and forgotten. As far away from you as the east is from the west.

Dave

[sincerely appreciative]

Thank you very much ma'am, you're a very sweet person. It's easy to see where Cecelia gets her good heart and love of people from.

Mrs. Barber

[smiles, flattered]

Thank you. I can also see why Cecelia thinks you're so special. C'mon, I'll introduce you to Pastor John—he's very nice.

Mrs. Barber

[walking toward the pastor]

Pastor John, this is Cecelia's friend, Mr. Dave Tripiciano. He's the school band director at Green Valley, where she went to high school. They met at the college.

Pastor John

[smiling warmly, he eagerly shakes Dave's hand]

Hello there young man, good to meet you! If you're a friend of Cecelia's, you must be a pretty good guy. A school band director, hey? We've been looking for a choir and music director here at the church for months. The lady who used to do it moved away. Do you have any interest in donating your talents for God's work?

Dave

Sure, why not? It might be fun, and everyone here seems nice.

[Abrupt cut to a new scene]

[One year later] On the altar of the Barber's church:

Dave in a suit stands next to Cecelia, who is wearing a flowered dress. With them, are one bridesmaid and a best man, as they stand before Pastor John at the altar of the church. There are about thirty people spread out on Cecelia's side of the aisle, including her parents, her siblings, and some girl friends. But on Dave's side there are only three couples and four children. None of Dave's family is there, and neither are his parents.

Dave
[smiling at Cecelia]
I David, take you Cecelia, to be my wedded wife. To have and to hold, from this day forward, for better or for worse, for richer or for poorer, in sickness and in health, to love and to cherish, till death do us part.

Cecelia
[smiling at Dave]
I Cecelia, take you David, to be my wedded husband. To have and to hold, from this day forward, for better or for worse, for richer or for poorer, in sickness and in health, to love and to cherish, till death do us part.

Pastor John
I now pronounce you man and wife. You may kiss the bride.

Dave and Cecelia kiss tenderly to the applause of those present. Then they walk arm in arm down the aisle to the music of an out-of-tune piano. When they reach the back of the church, family and friends swarm around them to exchange handshakes and hugs.

[Fade to black]

[Three short vignettes that show Dave and Cecelia starting their life together as a married couple. During the following scenes there isn't any dialogue. But, again, we hear Dave's voice speaking as a "narrator," sharing his feelings and explaining what is happening. Some background music fades in and out as "filler" with the narration]

Dave

[narrating the scene below]

I served as the choir director at Cecelia's church for several years, but not because I cared about or wanted to serve God. I was motivated by pride. I saw it as another chance, and one more way, to show off my musical talents and impress people. . . .

Narrated Vignette #1: Dave stands before a small group of adult singers in the choir loft of the empty church. The streetlights shining through the windows tell us that it's evening. Cecelia is among the group of choir members, who are all holding music folders. Dave, smiling, is giving directions that we don't hear and a couple of people nod. He begins to move his arms and the choir members watch him intently as they move their mouths energetically singing with much enthusiasm.

Dave

[narrating the scene below]

During the first year of our marriage, Cecelia was in her senior year of college. She worked hard at being a loving, submissive wife while also attending classes and studying. She graduated from college with a degree in math the following spring. . . .

Narrated Vignette #2: – Several hundred graduates dressed in caps and gowns are seated on the stage of the college performing arts center. We see a close-up of Cecelia, waiting her turn in a line of grads who are filing past the podium to walk across the stage, shake hands, and receive their degree. As she walks across to get hers, Dave, her parents, and her many siblings cheer and applaud.

Dave [narrating the scenes below]
We bought a piece of land way up in the hills that had a very old trailer on it. We lived in the run-down trailer for a couple of years, then built a small, inexpensive house there. Soon, after our "dream home" was finished, our first child was born.

Narrated Vignettes: Dave and Cecelia standing on a country road as Dave points proudly to a faded, old-style trailer that sits on the property, overgrown with vines and brush.

[The same spot two years later] The trailer, now parked on a lawn and not overgrown, is being towed away by a truck.

[The same spot a few years later] Workers building a house in the spot where the trailer once stood.

[Months later] A small, basic ranch home with vinyl siding, nicely landscaped and surrounded by a lawn and garden.

[Abrupt cut to a new scene]

[A few weeks later, a hospital lobby at night]
Cecelia's mother, father, and several of her siblings sit in an almost-empty hospital lobby, looking concerned and tired; then Dave bursts through the door and runs toward them, with a smile.

Dave

It's a girl! It's a girl — and she's beautiful! Six pounds seven ounces. Tracy Tripiciano, Tracy Lynn Tripiciano!

Mrs. Barber

I like the idea of the Tr – sound starting both the first and last names. Tracy Tripiciano is a name that trips over the tongue.

Mr. Barber

[shaking Dave's hand]

Spoil her rotten Dave, and spend lots of time with her. They grow up fast you know. Way too fast, that's for sure.

[Fade to black]

[Two years later at the back of the church] After a Sunday morning service:

Dave holds Tracy, now a cute, dark-haired two-year-old, in one arm, as he shakes hands with the pastor. Cecelia is standing next to him, smiling and cradling a newborn that is wrapped in a pink blanket.

Pastor John

How's that new baby?

Cecelia

Her name's Nicole, and she's very sweet-natured.

Dave

[bragging]

A second daughter, my cup runneth over!

Pastor John
Will you take them huntin' and fishin' with you, Dave?

Dave
[making a joke]
Of course! Everyone knows that the main reason for having kids is to have lots of little hunting and fishing buddies!

Pastor John
I hear that the school band won the state championship.

Dave [proudly]
Yep, and that's not all! We've been invited to play at halftime for the Buffalo Bills' first home game next week on TV!

Pastor John
Congratulations! I'll be sure to watch!

Dave
I've applied for a band director's job in a much bigger school.

Pastor John
[disappointed]
Aw, you're not moving are you?

Dave
Well, if I get the job. **[passionately]** And why wouldn't I? I've paid my dues, and I've got a proven track record of building a championship marching band program in a school that never had any.

Pastor John
[sadly]
Oh well, I guess we'll have to find a new music director.

Cecelia
I don't wanna move Dave, this area's my home. My parents are here and we just built a new house. Our "dream house," remember?

Dave
This job could be an important stepping-stone to build my career, honey. We all have to make sacrifices in life.

[Fade to black]

[A series of very short vignettes that show Dave and Cecelia trying to establish themselves in a new area, and Dave working with the band]

Dave
[narrating the scenes below]
I uprooted Cecelia from her family and our new home against her wishes, and I gave very little consideration to her feelings. She followed me to another part of the state, where I took over a bigger and more prestigious band program. We attended church, but I didn't have a clue about living for Christ. I cared only about my hunting, my fishing, building my career, and making a name for myself. My son, Tom, was born, but I continued to live selfishly.

Dave and Cecelia are standing in the front yard of a house that is for sale, shaking hands with a realtor. After shaking their hands, the realtor reaches down and pulls the "For Sale" sign out of the lawn.

Dave marching proudly in a parade, next to a large marching band.

Cecelia working as a teller in a bank, greeting people who come to her window with a smile and counting money into their hands.

Dave and Cecelia attending church on a Sunday morning, and shaking hands with the pastor and others after the service.
Dave in a boat out on a lake fishing.

Dave camouflaged in a tree stand with a hunting bow.

[Fade to black]

[Five years later] The kitchen of Dave and Cecelia's home:

Cecelia
You can't mean that we have to move again! We're doing fine right where we are and you just finished renovating the house.

Dave
But it's a great opportunity! The chance of a lifetime! A bigger school with a huge, well-known, award-winning band!

Cecelia
The kids will have to leave their friends and change schools.

Dave
They're kids, they'll adjust. This is a chance for me to really make a name for myself. The kind of job that you dream about!

Cecelia

What about me! I've got a great job here at the bank and all the customers know me and like me. I'm up for a promotion, too.

Dave

You're smart and talented honey, you'll land another one.

Cecelia

I hate the thought of moving again, I finally made some friends here and we're just starting to feel like we "belong" at church.

Dave

Look, with the extra money I'll be getting from the new job I'll get you a beautiful new house and you'll be happy!

[Fade to black]

[A series of very short vignettes combined to make one narrated scene. This segment shows Dave and Cecelia moving to yet another new area]

Dave

[narrating the scene below]

We bought a house in the hills with several acres of land, on a back country road that passed through the woods. Because of a delay with the closing we couldn't move into it right away, so we had to rent a house in town for a month until we could move into ours. A young man named Josh had been renting a room there before we arrived and since we wouldn't be there long we agreed to let him stay and share the place with us. Cecelia seemed overly friendly with him and quite flirtatious, and I was jealous.

After we moved into our new house, I had no idea she stayed in contact with him. I was so wrapped up in my career, my hobbies, and my own self-centered world that I never knew she was having an affair with him that lasted for several years.

Narrated vignette #1: Dave and Cecelia are standing in the front yard of a modern ranch style home surrounded by woods on three sides. A realtor is pointing and waving his arms, as if he is describing the property. [Later] Dave, Cecelia, and their children stand in the kitchen of the house they are renting, meeting Josh for the first time. They smile and exchange handshakes as the young man gives them a tour of place.

Narrated vignette #2: [Two weeks Later] Cecelia, Dave, and Josh are in the kitchen. Cecelia takes a handful of ice from the freezer and puts it down the back of Josh's collar. Josh cries out with a smile as she laughs flirtatiously and runs playfully away. He chases her out of the room, laughing. Dave seems very jealous and upset by these antics. . . .

[Three weeks later] Cecelia and Josh are watching television together in the living room. They sit alone talking, laughing, and smiling warmly as they share a bowl of popcorn.

[Months later] Cecelia is shopping in a supermarket and Josh is with her, pushing the grocery cart for her. They stop and she points to a canned item on the top shelf. Josh gets the item down and places it in the cart. They smile at each other and continue walking.

[Abrupt cut to a new scene]

[Four years later] Dave's kitchen [The phone rings]:

Dave walks quickly into the room to answer the phone. [On the other end of the line is an average-looking overweight woman in her late thirties. The woman has the tone and attitude of a gossip or busybody. She speaks quickly and excitedly, as though she is sharing a very juicy and important piece of information with him]

Dave
Hello, this is Dave.

Gossipy Woman [eager, excited]
Dave, do you know where Cecelia is?

Dave
Uh, out shopping, why?

Gossipy Woman
Actually, she's with another man, it's that young man Josh.

Dave
[shocked and upset]
What! I don't believe you! Who is this?

Gossipy Woman
It's true, if you don't believe me ask your neighbors. It's been going on for years and I thought you'd want to know. They meet on Saturdays when she's shopping. I saw them together today in the supermarket. Go to the park outside of town and you'll find them.

Dave
[shocked, enraged, and then deeply hurt and sad]

[Fade to black]

[Thirty minutes later] A parking lot in a state park near town:

Cecelia's car is parked under a tree in a secluded spot in the far back corner of the parking lot. Dave, driving quite aggressively, sees her car there and swerves his car into the lot at high speed. Pulling up to the front of her car and slamming on the brakes, he jumps from his vehicle—not bothering to close the door—and runs over to her's. Josh is sitting on the passenger side of the front seat and Cecelia is lying down on the seat with her head resting on his lap. Her glasses are off and they are resting on the dashboard. As Dave jerks open the passenger side door, Cecelia screams in a panic. A scuffle ensues, with Dave pulling Josh roughly out of the car and punching him. Cecelia tries to restrain him as they yell at each other loudly.

Dave
So it's true! You are having an affair with Josh!

Cecelia
[surprised, screaming]
Uuhh, DAVE!!

Dave
Get out of that car, you home wrecker!!

Cecelia
DAVE NO!! NO! Don't hit him!!

Dave
[punching Josh repeatedly]
You've been messing with my wife long enough!!

Cecelia
[screams, terrified]
Aaeehhh!! Stop it!! Dave! Stop hitting him!! Don't hit him again!

Dave
[stops punching, then taunts]
There, I broke your glasses for ya! But you deserve a lot worse!

Cecelia
[gasping, panting, sobbing]
How did you find us!? Why did you come here like this!?

Dave
I'm your husband, remember?

Cecelia
All you've ever cared about is yourself!

Dave
All those times you said you were shopping—you deceitful liar! How could you do this to me and the kids?

Cecelia
Please just go! Go, and leave us alone!

Dave
I'll go, because I have an appointment. But when I get home you better be gone! I don't want to see either one of you ever again!

[Fade to Black]

[Later that night] The driveway of Dave and Cecelia's house: A very short, narrated vignette with Dave's voice as the narrator.

Dave
[narrating the scene below]
When I got home that evening, Cecelia's car was loaded with all of her things and also the children's clothes and toys.

Dave pulls his car into the driveway and gets out. Looking into her car he sees that it's loaded with all of her things. He is saddened as he sees she has also packed their children's things.

[Abrupt cut to a new scene]

[Moments later] Inside the kitchen of Dave and Cecelia's house:

Cecelia, teary-eyed and with a devastated expression, moves about the kitchen, gathering up a few last items.

[Dave enters]

Cecelia

[broken-hearted]
I'm almost ready to go.

Dave [sadly, quietly]
I see you packed the kids things, too.

Cecelia [sniffing back tears]
Can't take care of them by yourself, they'll have to go with me.

Dave
[thoughtful, disappointed]
I didn't think about that. Have you told them why you're leaving?

Cecelia
[desperately crying out]
Not yet. Oh Dave! Dave! Can't we talk?

Dave
What do you want me to say, that I forgive you? I'm devastated, Cecelia!

Cecelia
[sadly, looking downward]
I know it, and I know that I've done a terrible thing.

Dave
How long has this been going on?

Cecelia [hesitates, embarrassed]
Uhmm . . . Ever since he lived with us.

Dave [loudly, shocked]
FOUR YEARS!?

Cecelia
I'm sorry, I'm so sorry. I didn't mean for it to happen. I didn't think you'd ever find out. I wasn't doing it to hurt you.

Dave
[questioning, sadly]
I thought we had a good marriage; I've been faithful to you.

Cecelia
Faithful, huh! Well maybe, but you put everything else in your life ahead of me! Your career, your music, your sailing, your hunting, your fishing, your photography—you never thought about my needs, or what I enjoy.

Dave
You should've talked to me about it, if you had a problem.

Cecelia
I shouldn't have had to! When you love someone, spending time with them and considering their feelings should come first.

Dave [honestly]
I had no idea you were unhappy.

Cecelia
That's because you were always too wrapped up in yourself to think about it, let alone notice.

Dave
I'm sorry, hun. **[catches himself, then yells]** Wait a minute! Why am I apologizing to you, you're the one who's been unfaithful!

Cecelia
[sadly, and with a blank face]

I was unfaithful with another man. But you were unfaithful to your promises to love and cherish me, to put me first in all things, to be my best friend and partner in life, to honor and respect my wishes, my feelings and my needs . . . . . and to love me, the way that Christ loves the church.

[hopefully]
Since, in many ways we were both wrong, can you forgive me?

Dave
When you put it that way I pretty much have to. But how will I know that it will never happen again?

Cecelia
[sincerely]
It won't, I promise. Let's not throw away twelve years of marriage. Think about the kids!

Dave
Do you promise never to see him again?

Cecelia
[urgently]
Yes! Yes! I promise to never, ever, see him again!

Dave
Then I'm willing to forgive, and I'll try to forget.

Cecelia
[overjoyed, hugs him]
Oh thank you Dave! Thank you so much! You really *are* a good man.

Dave
From now on I'll try to be the world's greatest husband and father, you'll see.

[Abrupt cut to a new scene]

[The same night] Dave and Cecelia sitting on their couch:

Dave
[narrating the scene below]
After the hugs, the promises, and the apologies, we sat together on the couch and we cried and talked all night. Years of regrets, mistakes, and disappointments came pouring out as both of us shared our deepest feelings and we took the first step toward becoming best friends again. That winter I even took her on a romantic second honeymoon to the Florida Keys. I treated her like a princess for the next year, and it was by far the best year of our marriage. But then I sensed that something was wrong, as the storm clouds gathered again.

Dave and Cecelia sit on their living room couch talking, smiling, laughing, and crying together. Sometimes their debate is quite heated and at other times they simply hold hands and nod sadly in agreement.

The clock on the wall above them shows that they have been sitting there most of the night; at last, they kiss and go off to bed.

[Three months later] The two of them are sailing a boat on a beautiful sunny day somewhere in the Florida Keys. Later they lie on the beach, sunning themselves in their bathing suits.

That evening they are enjoying a feast of lobster and shrimp in a very nice "all you can eat" seafood restaurant.

[Two months later] In the basement playroom of their house: Dave and Cecelia are running and playing happily with their children, in some wild, crazy kickball game using scooters.

[Abrupt cut to a new scene]

[One year later] In the dining room of Dave and Cecelia's house:

Dave sits in a chair at the dining room table, talking to Cecelia, who sits in the next closest chair facing him. He seems very suspicious and quite concerned as he questions her.

Cecelia
[nervous]
What do you mean? What phone call are you talking about?

Dave
The kids said you locked the bedroom door and stayed on the phone for an hour, and you wouldn't let them come in!

Cecelia
[flippant]
It was nothing. I don't remember who I was talking to, and I know I wasn't on that long. It's none of their business anyway.

Dave
[now very suspicious]
Are you seeing Josh again?

Cecelia
[defensive]
NO! Absolutely not!

Dave
You promised to never, ever, see him again, remember?

Cecelia
[louder]
It wasn't him — I swear it wasn't!

Dave
[demanding loudly]
I think you're lying to me; I can see it in your eyes! Swear on your children's lives that you weren't talking to him!

Cecelia
[swallows, hesitates]
I swear on my children's lives . . . that I wasn't talking to him.
[Fade to black]

[Another series of scenes without dialogue, narrated by Dave]

Dave
[narrating the scene below]
Two days later, we woke up to a terrible rainstorm. Cecelia was late leaving for work that day so she ran off in a rush with only a quick goodbye as she hurried out the door into the downpour. Since the kids attended school where I worked, they always rode with me in the morning. As we made our way down the winding, country road it was raining so hard you couldn't see between the wipes of our wiper blades. As we came down a steep downhill grade and around a sharp bend, we were greeted by a horrible sight:

Cecelia's car had failed to negotiate the curve and had gone into the woods on the left side of the road, shearing off several saplings and coming to rest, twisted and mangled in the trees, some thirty feet from the roadway. The culvert was plugged with leaves, causing several inches of water to pour across the road like a river on that sharp downhill curve. Cecelia was going way too fast, in a hurry because she was late for work. When she hit deep water on a curve at that speed she didn't have a chance. Her car went airborne into the woods and came to rest there.

Panic stricken, I pulled over and jumped out. Nicole got out and started to follow me toward the wreck but it was pouring and I was afraid of what she might see, so I made her get back in the car. Cecelia's car had its front end wrapped around a tree and the roof was caved in. The windshield was gone and broken glass was scattered all over the hood. The front passenger side door was wide open, and she was lying on her back on the front seat with her feet sticking out of the open door. Her feet were already turning black and blue and she was making loud gurgling sounds as she tried to breathe. Her unused seat belt was underneath her.

[Early morning at Dave's house] Cecelia rushes to get out the door on time as a downpour rain beats against the windows. She gives Dave and the kids a quick kiss, and then rushes out into the rain, holding her coat over her head.

[Moments later] Dave and the kids are inside the car, driving down the dark, rain-drenched road. They drive slowly through the heavy, rain as the windshield wipers slap furiously and the raindrops beat loudly on the car's metal roof. Dave [driving] leans forward as he strains to see through the rain-washed windshield. He gasps and his eyes widen as he sees the accident. He slows the car and pulls over to the right side.

He jumps out of the car and Nicole gets out to follow him, but he shakes his head and motions for her to get back in the car. She makes a disappointed face, but respects her father's wishes and gets back in. Dave stands alone in the downpour near the edge of the pavement as water pours across the road and past him like a small river. His face is dripping wet as he surveys the horrific scene in the woods in disbelief.

Behind him is his rain-washed vehicle, still running with its lights on and the wipers beating. The dark silhouettes of his three children are inside. They are pressed against the fogged-up windows, peering out in the direction of Dave as he moves along the far shoulder toward the tragic scene in the woods:

The wrecked car has come to rest with its front end wrapped around a tree and the roof is caved in. The handfuls of broken glass scattered across the hood are all that remain of what was once the front windshield, and the front passenger side door is wide open. As Dave approaches the vehicle, he sees that Cecelia is lying on her back on the front seat with her head toward the steering wheel and her feet sticking out of the open door. Her feet are black and blue and her chest and body heave and convulse as she tries to breath. The seat belt that would have saved her is underneath her.

[Fade to black]

[October of 1990] Cecelia's funeral at Dave and Cecelia's church:

[This scene is narrated by Dave and accompanied by very sad music]

Dave [narrating the scene below]
To my great surprise and disappointment, Josh came to Cecelia's funeral. I took him outside and questioned him about their relationship and why he felt that it was appropriate for him to be there. I found out that she was seeing him again right before her death and that she had been on the phone with him the day that I questioned her about it. I was deeply hurt when I realized that she had lied to me when she swore on her children's lives.

I couldn't help but wonder if her death was God's judgment on her for that lie, and for going back to her sin after being forgiven; and after being given the chance to start a new relationship with a new and different husband who had learned from his mistakes.

[Inside a small country church] Dave and his children are dressed in black and seated in the front pew. Cecelia's siblings and her parents are seated in the row behind them and Dave's parents are also there. The pastor is speaking in front of a back drop of stained-glass windows and there's a closed coffin, surrounded by flowers, on the altar. Josh sneaks in the back of the church after the service has started, looking guilty and sheepish as he hides out in a back corner seat.

[Later] Dave and Josh are outside the church building alone, having a lengthy, intense, and passionate conversation. Dave is obviously upset but not arguing or yelling as he questions him. It's clear that Josh dislikes Dave, but he answers him politely, and with intensity.

[Later] Dave, his children, his parents, Cecelia's parents, and a few close friends [all looking very sad] are standing around the open grave at the cemetery; as the casket is lowered slowly into the ground.

[Fade to black]

Act 13

A New Man And A Whole New Life In Christ

[Three weeks later] Dave kneels in the woods, praying:

We're back to the same scene we saw earlier in a flashback. Dave is kneeling in the woods after hunting. This time we hear a more detailed version of his prayer as he accepts Jesus and pledges the rest of his life, his gifts and his talents to serving him.

Dave
Dear Heavenly Father, my heart is sick and my mind reels as I try to deal with not one but two of the most devastating things in my life at the same time! The tragic loss of my children's mother and the realization that I failed her so miserably as a husband that she had to turn elsewhere for love and friendship.

[Pauses; tears stream down his face]

I was a terrible sinner as a young man, and I've repented for those sins. But even now that I'm older, married, and active in church, I've still been incredibly selfish and self-centered.

[Pauses, then shouts] Lord Jesus, if you're really there and you can hear me, please come into my heart and fill me with your holy spirit. I've lived for myself all these years but now I want to live for you! Take my gifts, take my talents, and my life Lord; and use me in any way that you can. Here I am Lord, send me! I accept you Jesus, as my Lord and savior, and I dedicate the rest of my life to serving you and others.

[Fade to black]

[Weeks later] Dave is dressed in camouflage and sits with his bow in a tree stand, quietly scanning the woods for deer:

Dave
[thinking]
Soon after I said that prayer, asking Jesus to come into my heart and use me, things began to happen. First I felt something inside of me change and I began to think differently about what things in life are really important. Then it was almost as if I could hear God saying: "I hope you didn't say a prayer like that if you didn't mean it, because I'm about to take you up on that offer and send your life in a whole new direction—one that you can't even begin to imagine or believe."

[Abrupt cut to a new scene]

[A series of scenes without dialogue, narrated by Dave, that show him meeting, getting to know and then marrying Mary]

Dave
[narrating the scene below]
Now that God had softened my heart, I realized what I had lost and I missed Cecelia desperately. Lonely and in need of a companion, I probably would have started dating lots of women (which would have been devastating to my children), but God in his wisdom had other plans for my life and the perfect person in mind for me.

During the narration above, Dave sees a memory where he and Cecelia are running and playing happily with their children, in some wild, crazy kickball game using scooters in their basement.

Dave

[As the scene changes, he continues narrating the scenes below]
A beautiful young widow, named Mary, with two young children heard of my loss through one of my colleagues and reached out to me. She had lost her husband in a plane crash a few years before and had become a Christian since then. She felt that God wanted her to write encouraging words to others who had tragically lost a loved one. We met, became friends, and began a dating relationship. Besides being strong, compassionate, sensitive, and intelligent, she was attractive and ten years younger than I was. Needless to say, I was surprised and very flattered that a woman like her would be interested in me.

Narrated vignette #1: Dave is standing on the front porch of a well-maintained, two-story colonial home ringing the doorbell. A strikingly attractive younger woman with long straight hair answers the door, smiling warmly.

Once inside the house she introduces him to her two small children who are watching TV in the living room while munching on pieces of pizza. Dan is an outgoing kindergarten boy with curly blonde hair and blue eyes. His younger sister, Lauren, is a cute little preschool sprite with short, straight, light brown hair and big brown eyes.

Narrated vignette #2: [A week later] Dave is sitting next to Mary in a movie theater. Lauren sits on her lap, eating popcorn, and Dan sits next to her, smiling at the antics of the animated characters on the screen.

Narrated vignette #3: [Two months later] Dave and his three children are having dinner at Mary's house with her and her two children. They are all seated at her large dining room table, eating Mexican food, talking and smiling happily.

Dave

[narrating the scene below]

We grew to love each other and each other's children, and our children gradually became good friends with each other. We were married a year and a half later at a Baptist church we had been attending. Mary was a beautiful young bride, and I praised God for bringing us together.

Vignette #1: [Dave and Mary's Wedding - Valentine's Day 1992] Dave, his father, Dan, and Tom are dressed in tuxes and stand at the altar of a large church. Dave's daughter Nicole walks down the aisle dressed in a bridesmaid dress. As Nicole reaches the front, Tracy starts down the aisle from the back, wearing the same dress. Finally, little Lauren as the "flower girl" comes down the aisle, strewing petals from her basket onto the floor. The congregation stands as the organ begins the bridal music. Mary — stunning in her gown and veil — is escorted down the aisle by her father.

[Abrupt cut to a new scene]

Later in the ceremony, Dave and Mary turn toward each other to exchange their vows. They face each other, standing in front of the pastor, smiling:

Pastor

Since you have come here of your own free will to unite in holy matrimony, I ask that you now recite your wedding vows.

Dave

[smiling at Mary]

I David, take you Mary, to be my lawfully wedded wife, my best friend, my faithful partner, and my lover from this day forward. In the presence of God and our family and friends, I offer you my solemn vow to be your faithful partner in sickness and in health, in good times and in bad, and in joy as well as in sorrow.

I promise to love you unconditionally, as God loves the church; to help you achieve your goals; to honor and respect you; to laugh with you and cry with you; and to cherish you for as long as we both shall live.

Mary

[smiling at Dave]

I Mary, take you David, to be my lawfully wedded husband, my best friend, my faithful partner, and my lover from this day forward. In the presence of God and our family and friends, I offer you my solemn vow to be your faithful partner in sickness and in health, in good times and in bad, and in joy as well as in sorrow.

I promise to love you unconditionally, as God loves the church; to help you achieve your goals; to honor and respect you; to laugh with you and cry with you; and to cherish you for as long as we both shall live.

Pastor

By the authority vested in me by God and the state of New York, I now pronounce you man and wife. You may kiss your bride.

Dave and Mary kiss tenderly and then turn to walk down the aisle to loud, traditional organ music. Their children, Dave's father, and the other bridesmaids follow. They get handshakes and hugs from family and friends when they reach the back of the church.

[Fade to black]

[Another series of short vignettes, narrated by Dave]

Dave
[narrating the scenes below]
I'd love to say: "and then we lived happily ever after," but I can't, because it wasn't until after the wedding that we realized how difficult our blended family situation really was. We were two deeply wounded adults, ten years apart in age, from different "eras" and completely different backgrounds. We had very different personalities, experiences, philosophies, and expectations, and we were trying to raise two sets of hurting, wounded children that were used to different styles of parenting, and had been brought up in different households. We made every mistake that parents can make as we struggled with the hurts of the past and our expectations for each other. Sometimes in a moment of frustration we allowed our anger and disappointment to come out, arguing loudly and attacking each other verbally.

But this time it was different. This time God was in the marriage; maturing us, guiding us, directing us, healing us, and holding us together. In spite of my sinful, selfish past, He loved me enough to give me the perfect woman to be my soul mate and best friend. Through the years we've "sharpened" each other like iron sharpens iron, and our family has matured to the point where we think of all five children as our own.

Vignette #1: It's a beautiful, sunny day. Dave and Mary are taking a walk. They are walking hand in hand and smiling.

Vignette #2: [Some time later] Nicole is picking on Dan and he starts to cry. Mary begins to reprimand her but Dave intervenes. Dave and Mary face off, pointing and arguing angrily; as an intense shouting match escalates.

Vignette #3: Dave, Tom, and Dan are packing books in boxes in the garage to be stored in the attic. When Dave isn't looking, Dan throws a book that accidentally hits him in the side of the face, startling and hurting him. Dave, believing it was a deliberate, disrespectful act reacts in anger, spanking him soundly. Dan runs to Mary crying and shaking with fear and she embraces him tenderly. Mary is enraged at Dave; she storms out to the garage where she and Dave begin another loud, heated argument about disciplining the children.

Vignette #4: [Some time later] Dave is building a tree fort in the back yard with Dan. He smiles at the boy and guides his hands as he allows the youngster to cut a board and then nail it into place.

Vignette #5: [Some time later] Tom runs into the house all excited with a handful of wilted wild flowers he's picked in the yard. With a big smile he proudly offers them to Mary. She smiles happily, makes a big deal over them and puts them in a vase of water on the dining room table.

Vignette #6: [Some time later] The children are older and the whole family is on a sailboat, sailing on a small lake. The kids are wearing life jackets and everyone is smiling as Dan proudly

steers the "ship." Then moments later, Dave is motoring the sailboat and pulling Tom and Dan along behind it on a large, inflatable inner tube.

Dave

[narrating the scene below]

Soon after we were married, I stepped down from my position as the director of a large marching band to take a low-key job as an elementary band director. I know it was God's hand and no coincidence that this school district happened to have a video production studio. There I learned how to edit and produce a professional video without ever having to go back to school or take a class in video production. Wildlife photography and videography had been one of my hobbies for many years.

The first way that God used my gifts was to allow me to produce several unique Christian videos. Some of them combined wildlife scenes with scripture verses, Christian background music, and nature sounds. Others had trophy game animals and hunting tips in addition to a salvation message geared toward outdoorsmen who might never set foot in a church.

Dave is seated in front of a TV monitor at a desk that contains video editing equipment, sound equipment, and other high-tech devices.

He is wearing headphones and speaking into a microphone as he flips switches and turns knobs. He is intensely focused on the TV screen, which has images of a deer with large antlers moving across it. He smiles and nods happily as he works, clearly enjoying himself.

Dave
[narrating the scene below]
After one year at that school, my teacher's pension was secure, so I left teaching to produce more videos and start an outreach ministry for hunters and outdoorsmen.

I named it "My Father's World" to honor my heavenly father who created all things and my earthly father who shared his love of hunting and the outdoors with me. To promote my videos and reach more hunters, I set up displays at outdoor shows around the country. My TV sets, showing stunning footage of trophy game animals, drew hunters in, and as they stood there admiring the big bucks; I was able to witness to them and tell them how God had changed my life.

[The inside of a large convention center]

A huge "outdoor show" is going on. There are fishing boats on display, a man drawing back a hunting bow and other men handling and admiring guns. There are mounted game heads on the walls and the building is crowded with men and women wearing hunting hats and camouflage clothing. They are milling around, walking past and browsing at hundreds of different displays. Some booths advertise guide services, hunting trips, and taxidermy, while others are selling everything from arrows to canoes.

Dave is dressed in a camouflage shirt, and standing under a sign that reads: "My Father's World" Outdoor Videos in bold letters. On his right and left two TV sets show colorful footage of deer and elk. A soothing instrumental version of "Amazing Grace," mixed with bird sounds, comes from one of the TVs, filling his booth and the surrounding area with music. He stands behind

a table with a wildlife tablecloth that is filled with his videos, business cards, literature, and tracts that feature famous hunters and fishermen. Two hunters stand at his display, smiling and pointing as they watch his videos. One of them approaches Dave:

Hunter
[pointing at TV]
You sure have some beautiful bucks in your videos! Is that gospel music you're using for the background music?

Dave
Yes it is! The good Lord loved me enough to save me and change me, so I'm gonna advertise for him every chance I get.

Hunter
You're a lucky guy to be able to film bucks like that and produce hunting videos for a living.

Dave
[smiling]
It's not luck. Ever since I dedicated my life to serving God, he's blessed me in ways that seem too good to be true. Here, take these with you. **[Hands him some tracts]** These are the true stories of famous hunters and fishermen who are Christians. They tell all about how their lives were changed and blessed after they invited Jesus into their hearts and started to live for him. Read 'em, it's pretty powerful stuff!

Hunter
Hey thanks man, you're a good salesman! Actually, I go to church once in a while myself with the wife and kids. We have a game dinner at our church every year in January and they're always

looking for a guest speaker. Do you have a business card? I'll give it to my pastor. You and your videos would be a big hit.

Dave
[handing him a card]
Sure, there you go; I'd be honored to come. I've been doing that a lot lately and I don't charge anything for coming either.

[Abrupt cut to a new scene]

Dave is editing a video at his desk. The phone rings.

Dave
[answering the phone]
Hello, "My Father's World."

Gray-haired Man
I'd like to speak to Dave Tripiciano.

Dave
This is Dave speaking.

Gray-haired Man
Hi Dave, this is Pastor Larry from the Bradford Assembly of God church. Some of the men from our church heard you speak last year over in Clearfield and they tell me that you've got some beautiful videos and a very touching, powerful story. Were having our annual sportsmen's outreach dinner on February 12th, and I wondered if you'd be available to come that day and be our guest speaker?

Dave
[flipping through a calendar]
I'd love to, if I'm free that day. Hold on a minute while I check the calendar. **[Stops flipping . . . reviews his calendar]** I've got one the week before and one the week after, so God must want me at your church that weekend. Shall I put it down as a definite date?

Pastor Larry
Yes, please do, and I'll send you some directions and more information about it when it gets closer. It sounds like your story is exactly what some of the men in our congregation need to hear.

[Abrupt cut to a new scene]

[Several months later] Inside the sanctuary of a large church:

Dave is giving a hunting seminar. He stands behind the pulpit, speaking into the microphone wearing a camouflage shirt and jeans. The room is filled with outdoorsmen, many of them dressed in hunting apparel. There are also quite a few women and children.

Dave
Whenever we go afield, our greatest responsibility is to conduct ourselves in a way that shows hunters as safe, ethical, responsible sportsmen and women. We need to practice with, and sight in our gun or bow for pinpoint accuracy, and take only the shots we know we can make, so we harvest game quickly, cleanly, and humanely. It's also important that whatever fish or game we take is used for food — either by our family or someone else who needs the meat, and will enjoy it. Many states now have a venison donation program where the meat from your deer is given to needy families,

or goes to feed homeless people in soup kitchens, missions, and homeless shelters.

[The same program a little later] Dave is still at the pulpit speaking:

As he wraps up his hunting seminar, his tone changes. He speaks slowly and clearly, with great weight and intensity as he shares his story. The audience is now very attentive and very quiet.

Dave

The next part is hard for me to share, but I need to share it, so you can see that God can forgive, change and use the worst sinner.

[A few moments later, loudly and passionately]

. . . A man who was divorced twice and remarried a third time before he was twenty-six years old. . . . A man who could run out on a little boy who called him "daddy" just so he could be with a new and exciting younger woman. . . . A man who was so self-centered and self-focused that his wife had to turn elsewhere for love and attention . . .

Does God love and forgive even a man like that? The answer is YES, my friends — a resounding YES. He not only loves and forgives him; but he will change him, use him, and bless him beyond his wildest dreams! He poured out his blood and died an agonizingly painful death just to wash away my sins and yours, and He loves even the worst sinner among us more than we could ever imagine.

. . . The Bible says: If any man be in Christ he is a new creation: old things are passed away and all things have become new. I know that verse is true! . . . Since he saved me, I really am a new creation!

A new and different human being! He's changed my heart so much that I can't even understand how I could have done some of the things I did as a young man! I know that all things have become new in me because I'm no longer capable of doing the things that I did back then, and I can't even understand how I could have possibly done them! I hate "the man I was" and I'm glad that I am a new "creation."

What are your talents and gifts? Have you asked God to use them? Have you invited Him into your heart and surrendered your life to Him? When you do, He will bless you and use you in ways you can't even imagine.

[Later that night] Outside the church, after the program is over:

Dave's SUV is backed up to one of the exit doors of the sanctuary. The door is open, illuminating the back of Dave's car. His vehicle has been lettered for his ministry, as a way to witness to other drivers and for advertising purposes. On the back window in large bold letters are the words "God Loves You", below that is the address of his web site: www.myfather-sworld.com. Dave comes out of the exit door carrying boxes, followed by one of the men from the church that is helping him carry his stuff out to the car.

Man from Church

That was a great program Dave. You really do have an amazing story to share. Thanks for sharing it all, even the hard stuff. There were a lot of men here that don't attend our church. I think you may have touched some hearts tonight. Thanks a lot for coming.

Dave
[shaking his hand]
Thanks for having me Rich. You've got some good men in this church. It was a blessing to be here and nice meeting you.

[Fade to black]

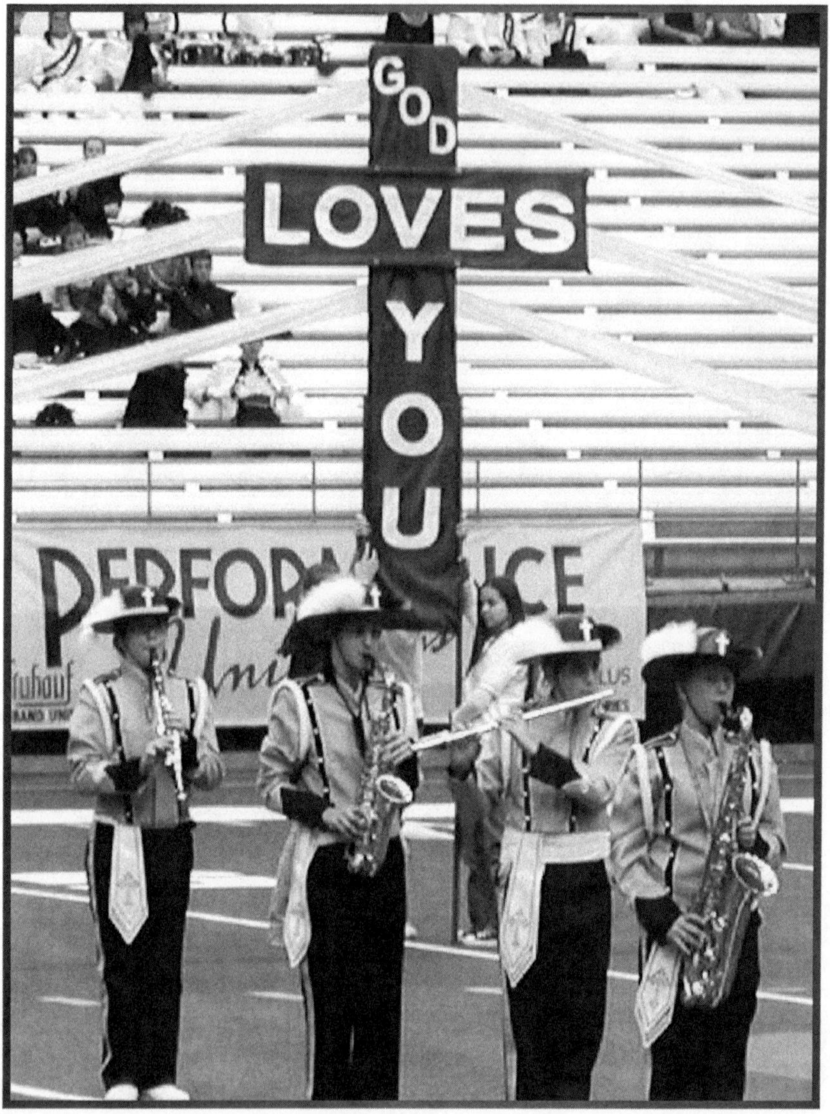
GOD
LOVES
YOU

Act 14

The Band Program Blessed And Used By God

[Three years later] The Lima Christian School band in a parade:

Dave

[narrating, with the sounds of the band heard in the background]
Without a doubt, God had used me to produce eight videos, and He was using my tragic life story to touch the hearts and lives of men wherever I spoke. But just when I thought I had Him figured out, He sent my life in a whole new direction and used my gifts and experience as a band director in new and exciting ways by bringing me to Lima Christian School.

Vignette #1: An aerial shot of the Lima Christian School band marching in a parade; they're wearing their blue-and-white uniforms. The camera drops down quickly and closes in on the band as a close shot of row after row of band members pass beneath it. They are playing a marching band arrangement of "How Great Thou Art" with lots of power and much intensity and pride. Dave marches proudly beside the band, smiling as he gives a thumbs up to parents who smile and wave from the curb as the band passes by.

[Abrupt cut to a new scene]

Vignette #2: The Lima Christian School band is giving a powerful, spirited, uplifting performance in a different parade. [no narration; just the sound of the band]

Two girls carry a large blue banner in front of the band as they march down the street. In large white letters, the banner reads: Lima Christian School "Marching Saints" To God Be The Glory.

Following the banner girls, comes the flag corps, twirling and slapping their flags aggressively. They carry themselves well and are perfectly in synch as they execute a difficult flag routine. Their rectangular white flags are trimmed in blue around the outside and have large blue crosses centered on them.

Next comes the band, sounding very full and powerful as they play an up-tempo arrangement of "*Power In The Blood.*" As they approach the reviewing stand, the crowd begins to clap and cheer for the sharp-looking, great-sounding group. As the band passes the stand, they begin a side to side step with their bodies and instruments facing the crowd. As they side step gracefully past us in perfect choreography, they are playing a soft, plaintive arrangement of "Jesus Loves Me," which features the flute section. Once past the reviewing stand, they turn to again, face down the street in the direction of march. They move away playing a slow, full-sounding arrangement of "How Great Thou Art." When they reach the final chorus they spin back around, aiming their instruments back toward the reviewing stand, and march backwards; playing the finale with great power and gusto in a slow, dramatic tempo. The girls in the flag corps have fallen back, and have come to a position behind the band. They are standing around a large, flat object that some of the band parents have placed in the center of the street, right in front of the reviewing stand.

As the band plays the last few lines of the song slowly and dramatically, the girls in the flag corps lift a giant cross, standing it upright in the middle of the street. The huge cross is made of dark blue fabric on a frame of lightweight pipe and is close to twenty feet tall. It has the words "GOD LOVES YOU" emblazoned on it in bold white letters that can be read from two

blocks away. As the cross goes up, some of the girls unroll wide golden streamers, which are attached to the top and sides of the cross, out and down to the ground. The streamers simulate rays of light shooting out from the cross. As the girls stand proudly holding the cross up and stretching out each of their streamers, Betsy (the drum major) releases a live white dove from the foot of the cross; it takes flight and flies over the top of the band and off into the bright blue sky. As the band finishes the final notes of the song, she gives a dramatic military salute to the reviewing stand, as the crowd cheers and applauds enthusiastically.

[Abrupt cut to a new scene]

[Another series of short, narrated vignettes that combine to make one scene] This segment covers Dave's twelve-year career as the band director at Lima Christian School. It shows the growth of the band program during that time, and how God blessed and used Dave and the band.

Dave
[narrating the scene below]
I directed the band at Lima Christian school for the next twelve years. That was twice as long as I had stayed at any other teaching position, and I got far less pay than I had ever gotten before. I didn't mind, because I knew that when you work for God, He doesn't always pay you with money.

If you measured my income in blessings and satisfaction, I was a millionaire. I felt content and had joy in my heart, because I saw God using my gifts for His glory. I knew that I was doing what He had created me for and called me to do. He blessed the band program beyond my wildest dreams, allowing it to grow and flourish, and providing everything I could've ever hoped for.

He gave us not one, not two, but three different sets of band uniforms, all of them free or almost free as hand-me-downs from other schools. Each set was newer and nicer than the one before, and all of them just happened to be in our school colors. He provided a complete set of marching drums and all of the tubas, baritones, and other large instruments we could ever need, always at very low cost or free. We had two different sets of color-guard flags — each with a different Christian emblem on them, and some of the greatest parents in the world designed and built the giant cross we put up in every parade that said "God Loves You." We also got a trailer to haul our uniforms, band instruments, and equipment, and we had it professionally lettered with our school name, our band's name, and large Christian fish emblems.

During the years I was there, the band program grew from thirty students to a hundred and sixty. So the school built an addition with a stage, and a large state-of-the-art band room with lots of shelves for uniform and instrument storage. The marching band's mission was to touch lives for Christ, so our main focus wasn't winning trophies and awards. But even so, we began to run out of space to display all of the first-place trophies we won, many times placing ahead of some of the largest public school bands.

[Short vignettes without band sound or dialogue, only the narration (above) and touching music being played in the background to enhance the scenes]

Vignette #1: [Several short, very impressive clips of the band in action performing in numerous parades] Wide shots of the whole band, interspersed with close-ups of individual students with horns, drums or flags; playing, marching and performing with great pride and intensity. Shots of Dave, his students, and the parents all taking part in the performances: helping to carry the large cross down the street, loading and unloading instruments from cars, vans, and pickup trucks before and after parades.

Vignette #2: Over time the band uniforms improve in quality and style. The first uniform is a basic old-style blue jacket and trousers with white shoulder braids and a white sash. It includes a blue sparkle shako hat, with a tall white plume. The hat has a silver sunburst emblem on the front and a white cross is centered on it. A girl holding a flute is wearing this outfit before a performance and her mom is straightening her sash and adjusting her hat and plume.

The second uniform includes dark blue trousers with wide, light blue trouser stripes, trimmed with white piping. The top is a white, drum corps style blouse with a stiff blue military collar and blue waistband. On the right front side of the blouse is a wide, vertical light blue stripe trimmed with dark blue piping. On the vertical stripe, spelled out in white letters one above the other, is the word "Saints." The Aussie-style hat is black, with one side flipped up; on the front is a white cross, a white hat band, and a long white ostrich feather plume that lays on the brim of the hat. A boy holding a trumpet wears this uniform as he talks to some friends before a parade.

The third uniform includes tops and bottoms in light blue, with dark blue trouser stripes that have white piping. The jacket sleeves have dark blue cuffs, white piping and white scrollwork trimming the arms, and two white shoulder braids. The front of the short jacket is dark blue, trimmed with large buttons, white piping and several white cords that make horizontal lines across the chest, (as would be expected with any cadet-style uniform). The Aussie-style hat seen in the last shot is still being used. Two female clarinet players wearing these new looking, cadet-style uniforms, are lined up in the marching formation. With their heads and instruments held high, they pick their feet up marking time.

Vignette #3: A close up of the drum line, shows the snare drummers playing on six brand new white snares, followed by three quad tom players with new white drums that match the snares. Behind them come four matching white bass drums that graduate in size from smallest to largest. Each bass drum has a large blue cross that is centered on the brilliant white head with the letters LCS above it. The tuba player also has a large blue cross that is centered on the top front of the bell of his white sousaphone. Some of the flags have a large matching blue cross on them. While others have a blue Christian fish emblem on them. Then we see the giant "God Loves You" cross standing tall and looking very impressive in the center of the street with all of its streamers unrolled and stretched tight. The girls in the flag corps hold the cross and their streamers proudly. As they stand at attention they're surrounded by a crowd of people clapping, cheering and applauding.

Vignette #4: The band trailer with its doors open, as students and parents load equipment into it. It has two large back doors and a door on the front right side. The spacious white trailer is lettered beautifully with large, dark blue letters and artistic graphics. The wording on both sides reads: Lima Christian School "Marching Saints." There is a Christian fish emblem with a cross going through the center of the fish, and rays of light radiating from the cross, on the front and both sides of the trailer; and on one of the back doors are the words "God Loves You".

Vignette #5: A construction crew building an addition to the school to house a large band room.

Vignette #6: Dave rehearsing the band in the beautiful, well-lit, spacious, state-of-the-art room. Several white tubas with crosses on them hang on hooks along the side wall, and the entire back wall of the room is a series of storage shelves and open closet space filled with drums, instrument cases and uniforms.

Vignette #7: Betsy, in uniform, is carrying and showing off a large band trophy to the kids and parents after a parade. She proudly brings it over to Dave who holds it up, smiling. In the final shot of this scene, the camera pans down a long band room shelf that is filled with a great number of impressive trophies.

[Fade to black]

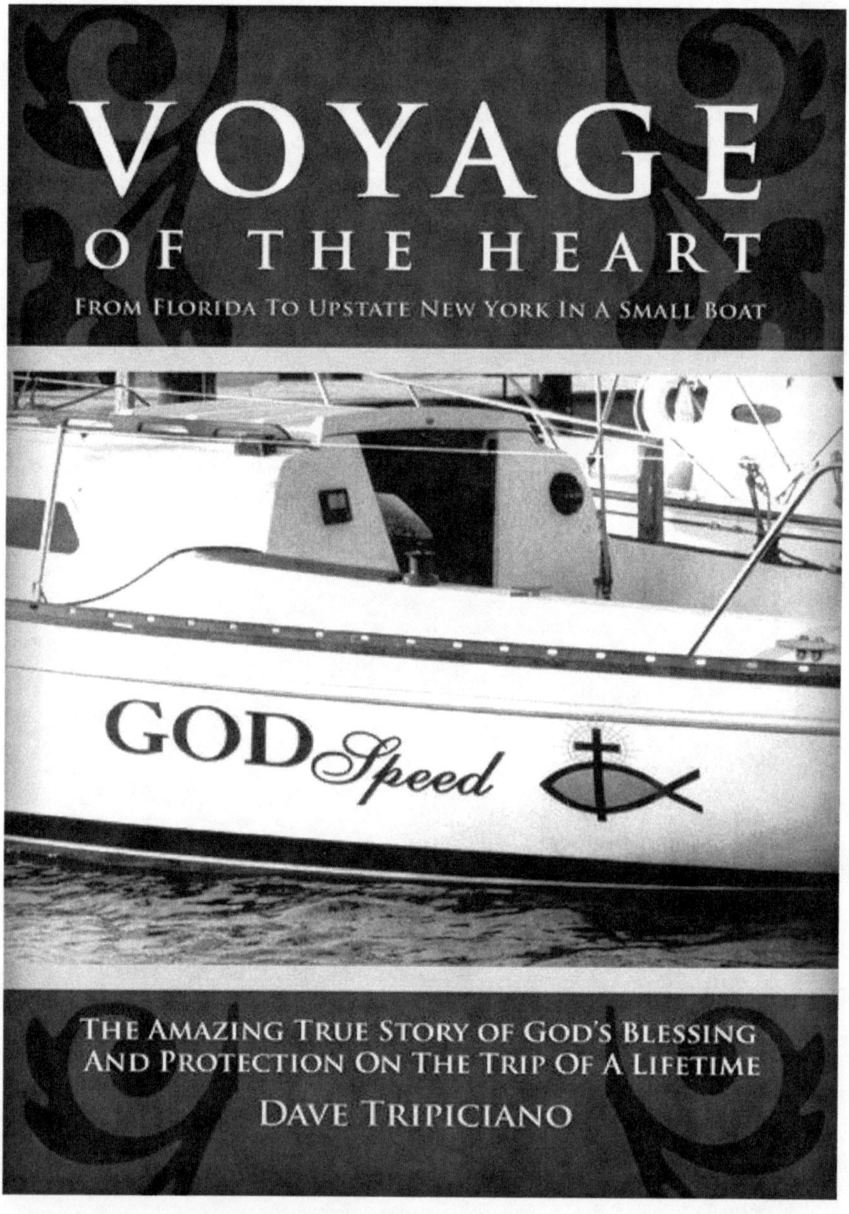
VOYAGE
OF THE HEART
FROM FLORIDA TO UPSTATE NEW YORK IN A SMALL BOAT
GOD Speed
THE AMAZING TRUE STORY OF GOD'S BLESSING
AND PROTECTION ON THE TRIP OF A LIFETIME
DAVE TRIPICIANO

Act 15 •

Sailing Through America And Writing A Book

Dave, alone on a sailboat, on a grass-lined river in the south:

Dave is sailing down a southern river, on a beautiful summer day. Wearing shorts, a T-shirt, and a wide-brimmed straw hat, he is sweating profusely as the midday sun beats down on him. He is on a river that runs through a wilderness area, surrounded by tall grass and marshlands as far as the eye can see in every direction. His boat has the name "God Speed" on the side in bold letters (big enough to read from quite a distance away). The word "God" is in large block letters and the word "Speed" is in script. The boat also has a large Christian fish emblem with a cross through it on both sides, exactly like the ones on the band trailer. A close-up of the flag fluttering at the top of the mast shows us that he is flying the Christian flag. He has his sails up as he moves slowly down the peaceful grassy river.

Dave

[narrating, as we watch him steering the boat]

In the summer of 2004, God allowed me to fulfill one of my lifelong dreams. He gave me a very nice, twenty-five foot Hunter sailboat at an affordable price, and allowed me to sail it through America, all the way from Florida to Rochester, New York.

Even though I was plagued by engine trouble, went aground several times, and found myself between two hurricanes, he was always with me and got me home safely. Living in the boat for over a month, I had lots of amazing adventures, and had the chance to meet and witness to many people along the way. When I got home, I sold the boat to get the money to publish a book about my adventure, called "**Voyage Of The Heart**". The book tells how God was with me, guiding me, blessing me, and protecting me along the way. It's a true, day-by-day account, of all the things that happened on my voyage, that were far too miraculous and perfectly timed to have happened just by coincidence or chance.

[Abrupt cut to a new scene]

[Six years later] Dave - aboard a much larger sailboat:

Dave is again sailing a boat down a calm, quiet river. But it's a different river, in another state, several years later. This boat is much larger than his Hunter twenty-five. It's actually a sailing yacht by comparison, and has a wheel for steering instead of a tiller. One thing is the same however: The boat's name is "God Speed", and it's written in the same fonts, and has the same Christian emblem as his smaller boat.

Dave
[narrating, as we watch him steer the boat]
Some people thought I was foolish to sell my boat to get the money I needed to publish a book. But I knew that God would bless me, if I put His work before possessions and material things. So I told them: "It's His boat anyway, and He gave it to me. If I sell it to get the money for something that He wants me to do, and He really wants me to have one, then someday He'll give me a **huge** one." My book came out in 2006 and there are now thousands of copies of it in the hands of people around the world. A few years later, in the summer of 2009, God arranged for me to find and own a large sailing yacht, simply by trading a small boat for it.

[Abrupt cut to a new scene]

[A series of short narrated vignettes combined to make one scene] This segment shows Dave's struggles and triumphs, and God's hand of provision and blessing that allowed him to find, purchase, and refurbish a large, abandoned, sailing yacht in South Carolina, and then somehow miraculously get it home.

Dave
[narrating the scene below]
The boat was a 33-footer that was relatively new and had great lines. But it was sitting in a farmer's field in South Carolina for five years. It had been left there, abandoned and forgotten; with its windows and hatches open to the weather. It was full of water and bee's nests, and needed a new engine. It also needed electronics, interior carpentry work, plumbing, wiring, carpeting, painting, windows, fiberglass work, and lots of scrubbing, polishing, buffing, and TLC. That's the reason no one wanted it and the price seemed too good to be true.

The first time I went inside to check it out, I was swarmed and stung by dozens of bees. I almost decided that it was too much work (even for me), but being a dreamer, and a hopeless romantic, I couldn't resist getting a boat that big for almost nothing.

As I began to buy the parts I needed, I quickly learned that there is no such thing as an "almost free" big boat. But God must have wanted me to have it; because the blessings, the equipment, the people and the situations he sent my way were so amazing, so perfect, so miraculous, and so unbelievable that I would have had to be brain dead not to see his hand guiding, directing, and providing for every detail of the huge project. I spent a year driving back and forth to South Carolina to work on it during every school vacation, and when school let out, I spent part of a summer down there before it ever went into the water.

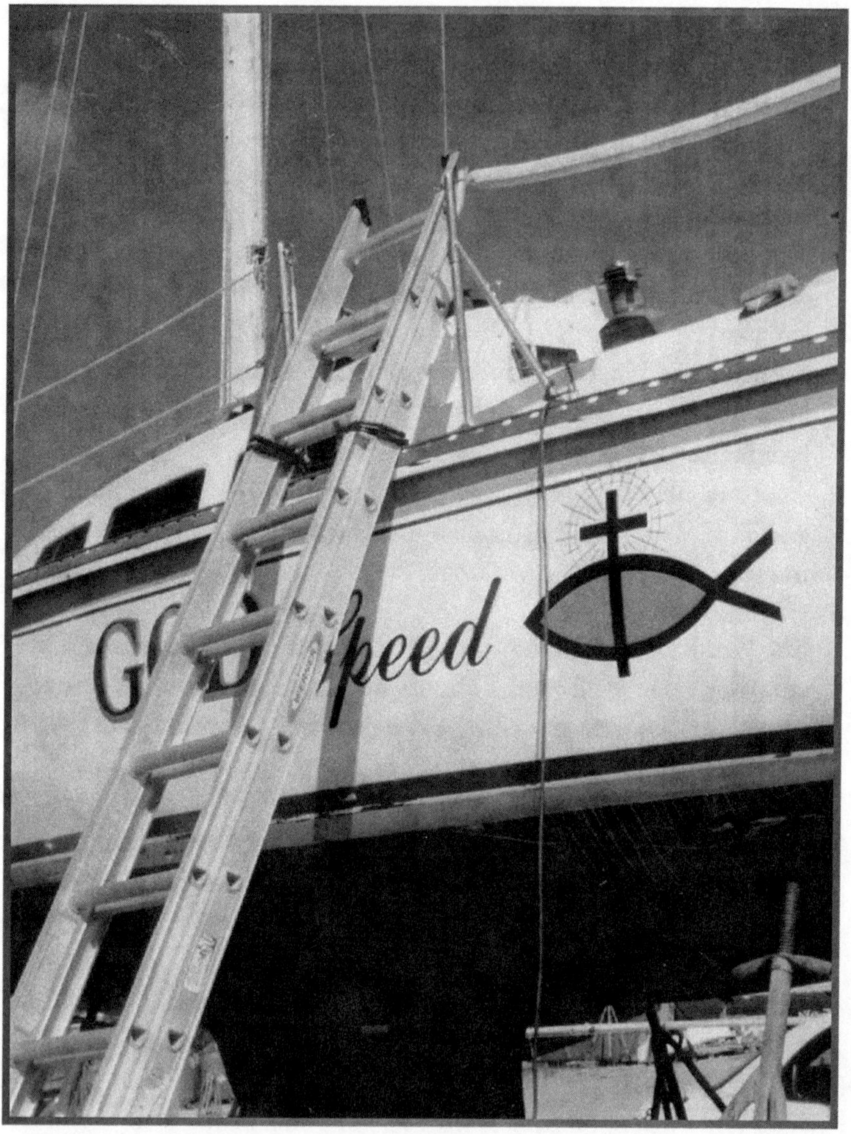

I had to store it in a boat yard in New Jersey for the winter, and it took me two summers to sail it home. But I believe that every stop was ordained by God. I met and witnessed to many different people along the way; giving quite a number of them signed copies of my book as well. Mary wasn't thrilled that I was away so much, but she was gracious and very patient with me, because she knew how long I had dreamed of owning a boat like that.

Vignette #1: A very large, attractive (but grubby) sailboat sitting on boat stands in a field next to a storage building on a farm near Charleston, South Carolina. Horses and cows are grazing near it. Dave climbs a tall ladder to board it. Once inside, Dave finds that it's filled with water, rotting wood, and bee's nests. Suddenly, he is swarmed by bees and begins waving his arms and swatting himself frantically as he runs out and scrambles back down the ladder.

[A bit later] He returns to cover the boat with a large tarp, and ties it down securely with bungies to keep water and pests out.

Vignette #2: Dave at a "West Marine" boat supply store. He has piled a large assortment of parts and supplies on the checkout counter. As the clerk tells him the total, his eyes widen and he shakes his head sadly as he slowly hands over his debit card.

[Later] Dave, inside the boat, installing the windows and carpet with a helper.

Vignette #3: Dave is in the engine compartment of the boat, tightening nuts and bolts on a brand new diesel engine. Another man who looks like a mechanic is advising him, and pointing at various parts as he shows him what to do.

Vignette #4: Dave, [with a helper] sawing wood, installing cabinets, and doing other carpentry work inside the boat. He is also staining and varnishing the interior woodwork.

Vignette #5: The boat is on boat stands in a boat yard, next to many other boats, both larger and smaller. Dave is covering it for the winter with a tarp and bungies.

Vignette #6: Dave is aboard the boat on a beautiful summer day. He is somewhere along the route on his voyage to get the boat home. He is motoring carefully into a dock, where a man is standing to help him come in. He tosses the man a rope and then jumps onto the dock himself. The two of them bring the boat gently against the dock and tie it securely. Dave shakes the man's hand, thanking him; then he begins to talk to him eagerly, pointing out into the water to explain his travel route. He steps back aboard his vessel, goes below, then reappears with a copy of his book and a pen. He signs it and gives it to the man, shaking his hand again. The man thanks him with a hearty smile.

[**Fade to black**]

Act 16 •

Beloved Teacher, Husband, Father & Grandfather

The Lima Christian School marching band performing in a parade:

In the downtown area of a good-sized city, the LCS marching band is in the middle of their performance, in front of the reviewing stand at a parade. A large crowd fills the reviewing stand and both sides of the street several persons deep. The band is doing a graceful side step, with their bodies and instruments facing the reviewing stand as they move slowly past the crowd. In the center of the band a girl stands atop a lightweight mobile stage, which is being towed down the street by an all-terrain vehicle. The small mobile stage has several large speakers and a sound system on it, and the girl is singing loudly and enthusiastically into a microphone. Her singing stands out clearly over the sound of the band, and she can be heard from several blocks away as her voice echoes off the downtown buildings.

Girl Singing
[loudly, with a smile]
. . . Jesus, Jesus, Je – sus . . . There's just something about that name . . . Kings and kingdoms will all pass away, but there's something about that name!

[Band continues instrumentally]

[Abrupt cut to a new scene]

Dave
[narrating the scene below, we hear the band in the background]
After twelve years directing the LCS marching band, I had reached retirement age, and after working with marching bands my whole life I didn't have another parade left in me. So I retired as the band director, but offered to become a volunteer "assistant" director and consultant, to help keep the band's ministry alive.

A wide shot of the "God Loves You" cross standing tall and looking very impressive where it's been erected; right in front of the reviewing stand at a parade. All of the streamers are unrolled and stretched tight. The girls in the flag corps hold the cross and their streamers proudly. As the girls stand at attention, the drum major releases a white dove from the foot of the cross; it takes wing and flies over the band and up into the cloudless blue sky; while the crowd lining the street cheers and applauds.

Dave
[narrating the scene below]
I've grown older, but my love for kids and working with them has grown deeper and more real. Unlike the young man who thought that being a band director was all about making a name for myself and winning trophies, I now know, that it's **really about** giving love and encouragement to a child, and the joy of seeing a kid have a positive experience and the fun of getting to play in the band.

Dave [Now in his sixties] sits in a chair playing a saxophone between two elementary school girls (who are also playing saxes). He nods as they play then puts down his instrument. He shakes his head and smiles as he playfully jokes with and teases the girl on his right about a mistake she made, pointing out something on the printed music. The three of them laugh and nod.

Dave [narrating]

I took a part-time position at two Christian schools where I get to work with students in grades four through eight two days a week. I guess I must've given the kids **too much** love and encouragement, because the band grew from twenty-five kids to sixty, and I was asked to teach at two more schools. Now I'm the busiest "semi-retired" guy I know, giving lessons and directing bands that include home schoolers three days a week at four Christian schools. In addition to having an outreach ministry for men, and speaking all over the country.

Vignette #1: Dave kneels on the floor, next to a tiny fourth grade girl playing a flute. The flute seems too big for her, and she holds it awkwardly looking very unsure of herself. But Dave, points out each note for her with a pencil; he nods smiling, encourages her, and coaxes her along as she plays. When she finishes, he jumps up shouting and cheering, waving his fists in the air and giving her a high-five as she laughs at his antics.

Vignette #2: Dave stands behind three elementary violin students who are seated in chairs in front of him. He is playing the violin with them, reading the music over their shoulders as the three youngsters move their bows up and down smoothly with confidence. As they finish playing, he walks around to the front to face them. With a big smile, he nods and applauds loudly, giving them two thumbs up.

Vignette #3: Dave is conducting a large, elementary/middle school band that is presenting a concert for the residents of a nursing home. The band is seated on one end of a large room that appears to be a cafeteria, while the audience fills the remainder of the crowded room.

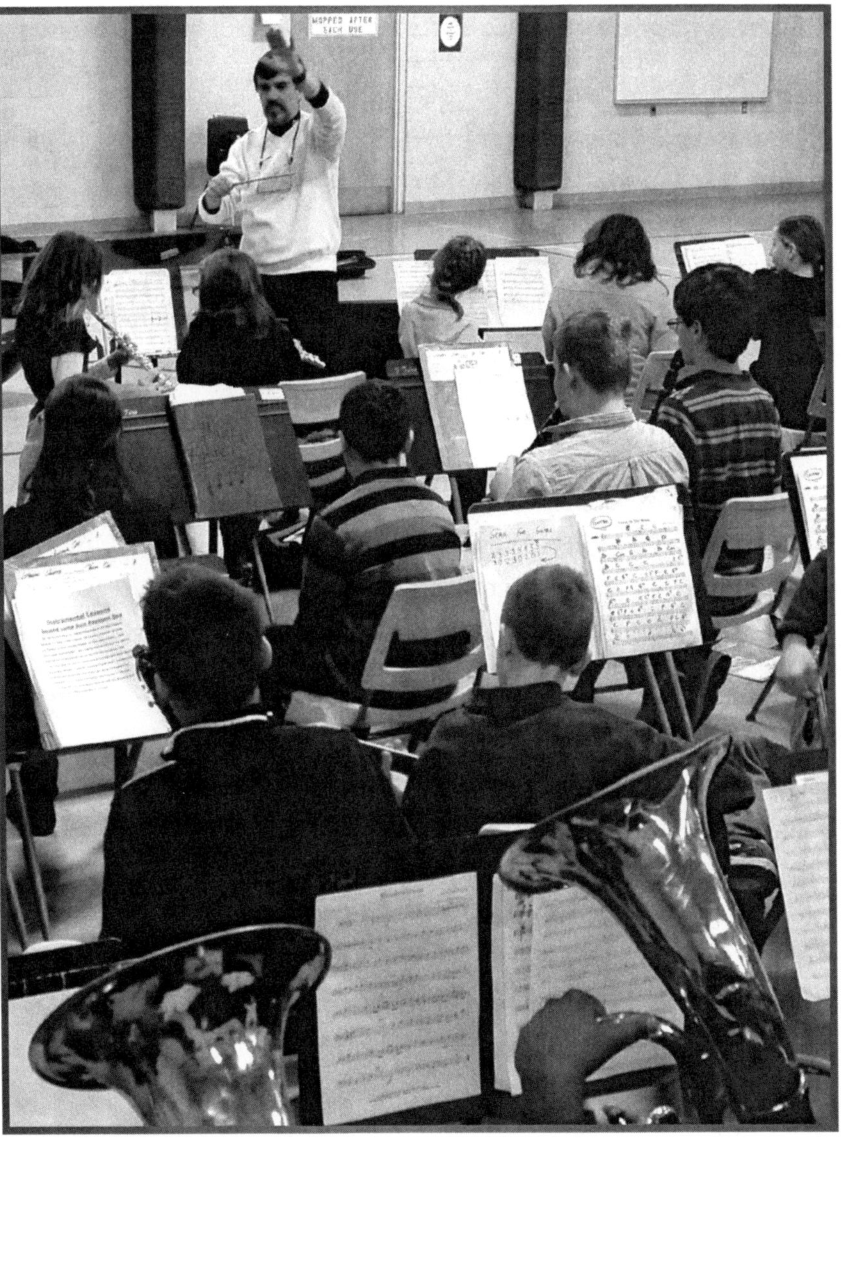
MOPPED AFTER
EACH USE

Most of the audience members are in wheelchairs and many of them seem too old or handicapped to even know where they are. After a musical selection, there are lots of smiles and some eager applause from some of the more physically able residents.

Dave
[narrating the scene below]
Now that I'm over sixty, I'm probably in the most rewarding and satisfying season of my life, because I have dozens of great kids who love me, count on me, and look up to me; and I get to be part of their lives, give them the gift of music, and watch them grow.

Dave is rehearsing a large elementary/middle school band in the small gymnasium of a Christian school. There are over sixty students in the group, including several violins in the front row and even a row of acoustic guitars. All of the students are sitting up attentively, looking at Dave as he gives directions. It's quite clear they like and respect him; as they begin to play, they seem to be enjoying themselves and giving their best effort.

Dave
[narrating the scenes below]
I started an archery club one night a week for our Christian school students and their parents during the winter months. We shoot at targets at an indoor archery range and keep score each week. The kids compete only with other kids their own age and ability level, and at the end of the season we have a party with lots of trophies, prizes, and awards. I usually break things down so that almost every child involved wins a prize for something.

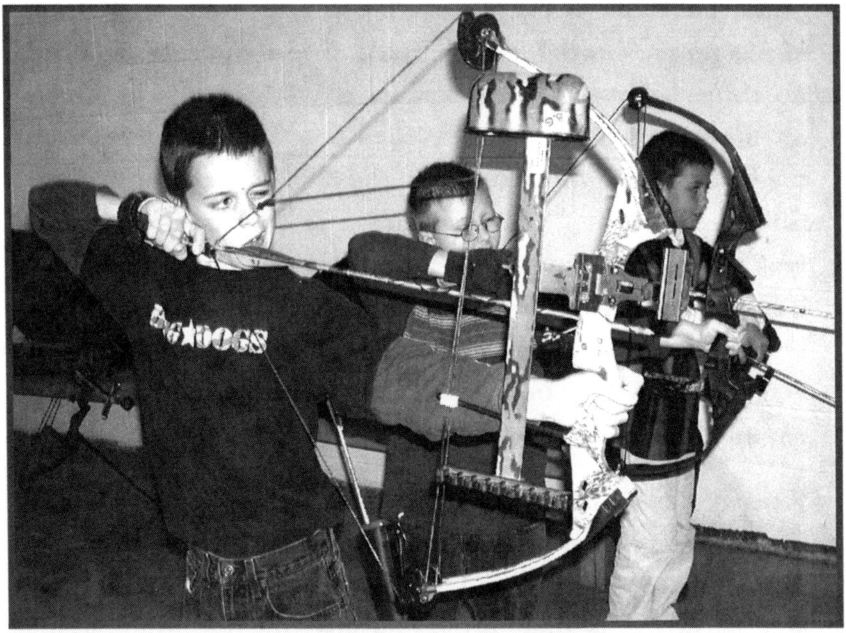

Vignette #1: Dave is at an indoor archery range with quite a number of students and parents; the students range in age from kindergarten through eighth grade. Seven students are lined up abreast, drawing bows to shoot arrows at bulls-eye targets on the wall and three-dimensional deer and bear targets on the floor. Several other students and parents stand behind the firing line, holding bows and arrows as they watch and wait for their turn to shoot. Dave kneels next to a first-grade boy, helping him pull his bow back and aim at a target. He helps him release the arrow, which hits one of the targets. Making an exaggerated, happy and excited face, he high-fives the smiling boy and musses his hair.

Vignette #2: [Another day at the same archery range] Dave is standing in front of a table filled with small archery trophies. Several dozen parents and students are eating snacks and holding drinks as they watch him give out the trophies and awards. He calls out a name and the first-grade boy that he was helping in the last scene squeezes his way through the crowd toward him. Smiling, Dave hands him a trophy and proudly shakes his hand.

Dave
[narrating the scenes below]
I found a church with a very small congregation just around the corner from my house. The beloved, older pastor is a loving shepherd with a sweet spirit, and he's an excellent example of Jesus, but the church had no musicians and no worship team. I helped out by attending services there on Sundays and banging on the piano to accompany the singing. Now that the church has merged with another small church, and we have more musicians, I play whatever instrument is needed to fill out the worship team.

Vignette #1: Dave is seated at a spinet piano at the front of a small church:

Dave plays the piano poorly, while a white-haired pastor stands behind a homemade pulpit and leads the small, older congregation in singing a favorite, old hymn of the faith. The pastor, a beloved man of God, is singing loudly and with gusto.

Vignette #2: [The same church four years later] The church has been remodeled and updated. The worship team now has two guitar players and an older woman playing an electronic keyboard. Two other women on the left side are singing into microphones and Dave is playing the bass guitar on the right, next to the keyboard.

[Fade to black]

[March of 2011] An American family is gathered around a large, old-style radio in their living room:

A family listens to the Christian radio drama "Unshackled." Loud, cheesy theatre style organ music cascades out of the radio, and then the voice of the narrator introduces tonight's episode:

Radio Announcer
Justified outrage, right? . . . Well perhaps, but the man in tonight's story was no stranger to infidelity, adultery, and divorce, until the day that his heart and his mind were "Unshackled." . . .

The loud, cheesy organ music crescendos again and the sound of the radio fades out, as the soft instrumental music of woodwinds, strings, and pan pipes playing "This Is My Father's

World," comes up. The family listening to the radio becomes wide-eyed and very attentive as the drama begins to unfold. But instead of hearing the radio, we hear Dave's voice speaking the narration below, over the soft, plaintive background music.

[Dave's narration is heard over the soothing background music]

Dave
[narrating]
In March of 2011, my life story was featured as an episode of the well-known Christian radio drama "Unshackled" and broadcast worldwide on Christian radio. This "old school" radio drama tries to simulate the classic radio serials that were broadcast in the days before television. Produced as a ministry of the "Pacific Garden Mission" in Chicago, the program uses actors to dramatize the life of a Christian man or woman who was delivered from a life of sin, and gone on to dedicate their life to serving the Lord.

[Fade To Black]

Dave [narrating the scenes below]
In 2011, I decided that since God had given me such a beautiful, large, sailing "yacht" and miraculously allowed me to refurbish it and get it home. I should somehow use it to bless others. Since my heart has always gone out to a handicapped child, I am planning to use my sailboat to somehow bless children with special needs.

In the summer of 2012, I hope to start: "Captain Dave's Boat Cruises" for handicapped and special needs kids. I would like to take orphans; and children with Down's syndrome, muscular dystrophy, cancer, and other handicaps or terminal illnesses for rides aboard the good ship "God Speed" along with their parents.

There will be no charge to the children and their families, but I might accept donations from churches, businesses, and charitable organizations to cover dockage, boat maintenance, and insurance.

We see the boat "God Speed," with both sails up, cruising on the calm, sparkling waters of Lake Ontario. The boat is sailing beautifully under a bright blue sky. At first we see it from above and from a distance, then the camera closes in to show the sails, the "God Speed" name and finally the person steering.

Vignette #1: There's a teen age boy with Down's syndrome at the wheel, wearing a life jacket and smiling from ear to ear as he steers the boat under full sail. Dave, standing behind him, has one hand on his shoulder and the other one pointing ahead, as he gives the boy instructions. The boy's parents are thrilled, as they sit watching from the cockpit seat next to him.

Vignette #2: [Another day] A middle school age African American girl steers the boat. She is bald and her empty wheelchair sits folded up off to one side. A special sling seat has been rigged up in front of the ship's wheel to support her. The girl's father and Dave are on either side of her, steadying her so she stays in the seat. She is wearing a specially designed floatation device as she steers the boat and smiles from ear to ear.

[Fade to black]

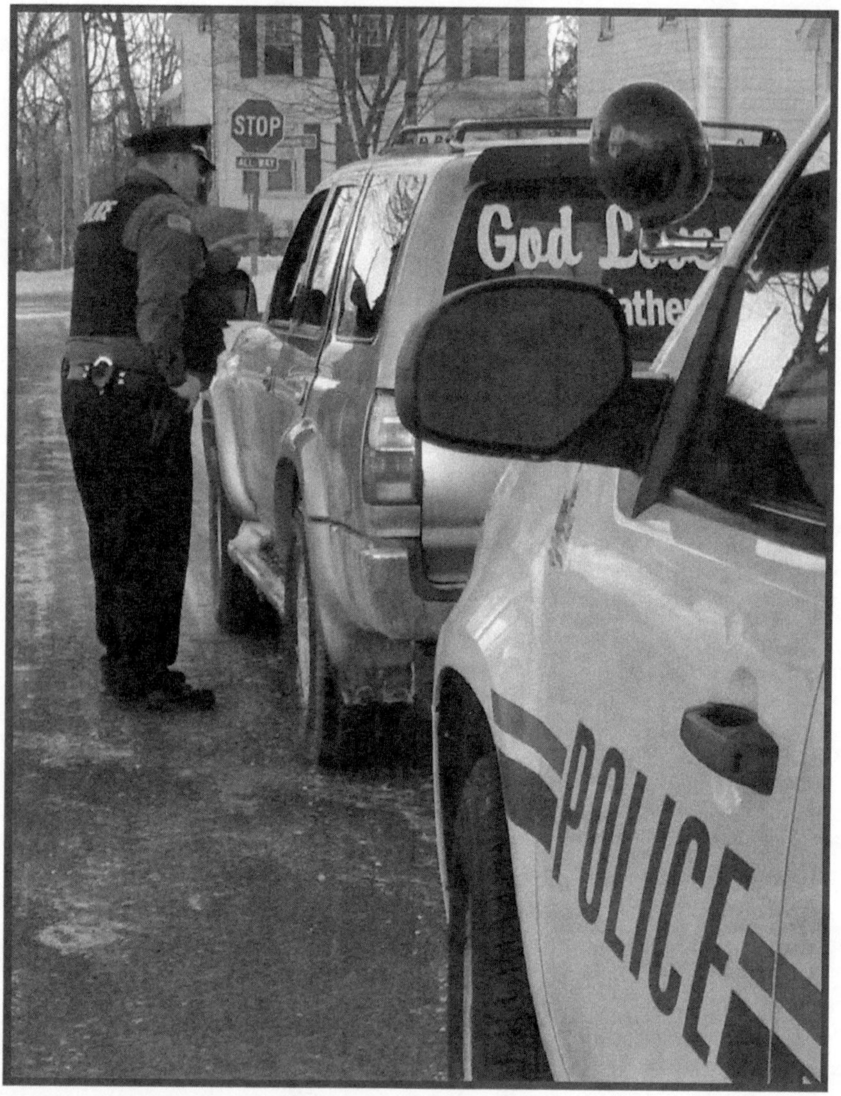
STOP
ALL WAY
POLICE

Act 17 •

Guess I've Touched A Few Lives Along The Way

[March of 2013] One Year After This Book Was Published

Dave is driving his car down the main street of a small town: He's alone in the car, steering slowly through a residential area past large older homes. Adjusting the volume knob he hums along with the radio then checks his rear view mirror. His face and body language tell us that he doesn't seem to have a care in the world, or be in any hurry. Smiling, he unwraps and pops a stick of gum into his mouth then continues to drive leisurely along, taking in the view on both sides of the street. As he drives he is nodding and drumming on the steering wheel with his hands to the beat of the music that is coming through the radio.

As he approaches the "downtown" business district, a police vehicle pulls out of a side street, and accelerates to move in close behind him. As he looks in the rear view mirror at the large, white, police SUV he starts talking to himself:

Dave

Oh Oh! This police officer came out of that side street pretty quick and moved right in behind me. It almost looks like he's following me. I sure hope not.

Dave looks at his speedometer, then nervously back into his mirror at the police vehicle behind him.
[he speaks again]:

Dave [staring into the rear view mirror]
I'm not speeding and I didn't go through a stop sign or red light.
[touching his seatbelt he looks back anxiously, then at his registration stickers]
I'm wearing my seatbelt, my registration hasn't expired, and I'm not due for an inspection until September. What did I do wrong and what is this guy up to? I'm gonna be turning right up there at the light, so I'll pull into the right lane <u>now</u> and see if he changes lanes too. Then maybe I'll know if he's following me.

An outside shot of both vehicles shows Dave's right turn signal come on and his car pulling to the right and into the right-hand lane. The police vehicle then signals and also moves into the right lane, pulling up even closer to Dave's car than it was before.

Dave [again looking into his mirror]
Oh no! I think he <u>is</u> following me and I have no idea why. He changed lanes right when I did and he's right on my bumper now.
[upset and <u>very</u> nervous]
What could I have possibly done wrong?

An outside shot of the police car shows all of the flashing multicolored lights on top of the vehicle coming on; and its headlights and turn signals also begin to flash.

Dave [looking into his mirror - frustrated and confused]
Oh great! I can't believe this! What did I do!?

Another outside shot of both vehicles shows Dave pulling over to the curb and the large white police SUV pulling over and coming to stop right behind him. A close-up of the police car shows the officer inside shutting off his flashers and calmly putting on his hat. After a pause of several seconds the door of the police vehicle opens and the officer gets out and walks slowly toward Dave's car. He is a tall, heavy set man with a round face and ruddy complexion.

Dave [nervously watching the officer come toward him in his rear view mirror] Holy cow this dude is big and he looks like he means business. He could probably break me in half if he wanted to, so I better not get him mad. I'll try to be really polite and respectful and maybe he won't give me a ticket.
[puts down his window]
But I still can't figure out what I could've possibly done wrong!

Another outside shot shows that the big boned police officer has almost reached the back of Dave's car. Wearing body armor, a side arm and a black "policemen's" hat, the large man is quite imposing and definitely someone who would command the respect of any driver he might pull over. As he walks toward Dave's driver's side window, Dave cranes his neck out to look back at him and speaks:

Dave [nervous and sheepishly]
W-W-Wh-What did I do wrong sir?

By now he has almost reached Dave's window and as Dave asks this question the man's facial expression changes from a stern scowl to a boyish grin as he answers: l

Officer [with a smile]
Nothin' coach, I just wanted to give you a hug!

Dave [smiling happily and greatly relieved]
Jeremey, oh my God Jeremey! You scared me to death man! I can't believe it's you!

Dave jumps out of the car to embrace Jeremey as the big guy (who makes Dave seem tiny by comparison) gives him a bear hug. It's a touching and somewhat comical scene as they embrace each other there in the street, while other surprised and bewildered drivers pass them and turn to stare.

Dave [with a smile as they pull apart]
You've grown up to be one big dude and you look very impressive in your police uniform. I think this is the first time I've ever seen you in uniform and on duty. Proud of you man, very proud to see you like this. Here I'm a nervous wreck thinkin' I did something wrong and was about to get a ticket, but instead I'm being pulled over by one of my best trombone players and favorite band kids of all time!

Jeremey [also smiling]
Can't let you drive through town without saying hello and giving you a hug coach.

Dave [smiling broadly, shaking his head and patting Jeremy on the shoulder]
Look at you, just look at you, Mr. "big-time" police officer. You sure have come a long way from that shy little fourth-grade trombone player that was in my elementary band. You've even come a long way from that high school trombone player that was in my jazz

band and marching band. Wow, so great to see you Jeremey, you look great man.

Jeremey
Great to see you too coach. You're looking pretty good yourself.
[elbows Dave smiling, teasing]
for an old guy.
[they both laugh]

Dave [an exciting thought occurs to him]
Hey Jer! Have you seen my new book? I gave you a copy of my first book a few years ago, but my second book just came out last year. It's all about the mistakes I made as a young man and my career as a band director.
[walks around to the back of his car as he says this and Jeremey follows]
You'll love it because it's about a lifetime of working with kids and bands.
[He takes a book from a box in the back of his car and begins to flip through it]
Check it out man it's even got pictures!
[He flips pages as Jeremey looks on, stopping at each picture and chapter title to point things out to him]
See that, pictures of the old coach working with kids just the way I used to work with you. Here are some pictures of my marching bands, and some pictures of my band kids posing with trophies that we won in a parade.

Jeremey [interrupts excitedly]
Some of the best memories in my life coach! Those are the things I remember the most from high school and that meant the most to me! Being in the marching band and going to all of the band

pageants! Winning first place trophies at almost every parade!
[shakes his head slowly with a smile remembering fondly]
I still remember how excited I'd get, as we came down the street in a big parade and started playing our music in front of the judging platform.
[grabs Dave's arm smiling and looks at him with an excited expression]
Remember the time we blew away all of the bands in our class at the Seneca Falls pageant of bands coach? I'll never forget it, we made a <u>clean sweep</u> that year and won first place trophies in marching band, concert band <u>and</u> jazz band!

Dave [nodding slowly and smiling]
Wow! You remember a lot of things that I don't even remember. You have no idea how much it means to me to hear all that stuff, and to know that I gave you some great memories and experiences that you still talk about.

Throughout this exchange, Dave is flipping through the open book pointing out the titles of each act and pictures that might be of interest to Jeremey. At this point the pages fall open to the beginning of act three, at a picture of Dave giving a flute lesson to two elementary school girls.

The title for the act reads:
"*Being A Hero In The Eyes Of A Child – Priceless*"
As Jeremey sees this title his eyes widen. With a serious and dramatic tone he points at the words as he proclaims to Dave in a loud voice:

Jeremy [looking at Dave & nodding seriously]
You were that for me coach! You were that for me and a lot of other kids. A hero.

Dave begins to tear up and makes no attempt to hold back. As tears run down his cheeks he shakes his head smiling, momentarily at a loss for words.

Dave [smiling as the tears flow]
Aw c'mon man, why'd you have to go and say something like that? Don't you know that old Italian men cry easy.
[Laughing through his tears]
Especially us sensitive musician types. Com'ere you big lug. . .
[Extends his arms for another hug and Jeremey embraces him again]
Thanks for making my day officer, you're the man!

Jeremey
No coach you're the man. You'll always be "the man" in my book.
[As he lets go of Dave an idea comes to him]

Jeremey
Hey coach! Can you use a trombone for the kids that you're working with now? I still have my trombone from high school and it's still in good condition.

Dave
Sure Jer, I can definetly use it. I'm always looking for good instruments to give to kids who's families might not be able to rent or buy one.

Jeremey
That's great cause it's just sitting in the closet collecting dust. If I give it to you I know it will go to a good kid and maybe give them some great memories and experiences like I had in band.
[pointing at some nearby houses]

My apartment's right over there. Follow me around the corner and I'll run upstairs and get it and give it to you.

Dave

That would be great. I can really use a nice trombone right now. Let me sign this book for you and you can bring it up to your apartment.

[Signs the book and hands it to Jeremey. Then they both get into their cars. Jeremey pulls out first, then Dave pulls out to follow the police SUV]

[Abrupt cut to a new scene]

A few moments later on another street just a couple of blocks away:

Jeremy's police car pulls over and comes to a stop in front of an older two-story home in what looks like an average blue-collar neighborhood. Dave's car pulls over and comes to a stop right behind the police vehicle.

The door of the police car swings open and Jeremy jumps out. Still in full uniform he runs across the street and around to the side of the house where he disappears into a doorway on the side porch. In less than a minute he emerges from the same door carrying a trombone case. Dave sees him coming and steps out of his car. Jeremey runs toward him smiling and hands him the trombone.

Jeremey

There you go coach it's like new. I bet some little kid will be thrilled to get this beauty!

Dave
I can't believe you're just giving me this, are you sure you don't want something for it?

Jeremey
Naw coach it's all yours. It's been sitting in the closet for years. Can't think of a better place for it to go. Use it to help and encourage a youngster like you did me.

Dave
Can't thank you enough man. You made my day! No I take that back; this is one of the best moments I've had in fourty years of teaching, so you just made my career! Running into you today reminded me that I've made a difference in the lives of a lot of kids.

Jeremey
You have coach, you really have. Probably more than you'll ever know.

Setting down the trombone case he gives Jeremey one more hug. As they embrace each other the two of them exchange goodbyes.

Dave
It was great running into you man. Thanks for everything. You were a great kid and you've grown up to be a great man. Proud of you dude! Keep in touch.

Jeremey
Great running into you too coach. Hopefully next time I won't have to pull you over to give you a hug. Call me if you need help with your boat cruises for kids.

Smiling happily Dave picks up the trombone, puts it in the back of his car and gets in, while Jeremey climbs into the drivers seat of the police car. With a wave and a honk they pull away from the curb, driving one behind the other to the corner, where they each turn in different directions to go their separate ways.

[Abrupt cut to a new scene]
A close-up of Dave driving his car, just moments after his encounter with Jeremey. Still slightly teary-eyed he is smiling broadly as he reflects on what just happened.

Dave [shaking his head in awe as he mumbles to himself]
I always knew that Jeremey liked me and loved band. But I had no idea that I meant that much to him or made that big of an impact on him. I think his father left their home when he was in kindergarten and his mother raised him alone. I guess he must've looked up to me as a father figure and mentor growing up and I never realized how much I actually meant to him until now.
[Pauses thinks a moment]
I just happened to run into Jeremey, but in 41 years of teaching I wonder how many <u>other</u> kids counted on me and looked up to me that way, even though I may never see them again? I wonder how many of my band kids think I made a difference in their life, or that band was the thing they liked best or remember most fondly from high school?

[He pauses, smiling broadly as the camera moves in for a facial close-up. As the camera closes in on his eyes, he starts daydreaming and reminiscing fondly about other kids he had the privilege of working with through the years]

The scene changes abruptly to a whole series of short scenes, that show Dave working with, helping or encouraging one student after another. Each one is then followed by a quick vignette that shows what that student is doing <u>now</u> as a mature, successful adult. Dave's voice narrates throughout this segment.

Dave's voice narrating the scene below: Now that I think about it, I <u>have</u> gotten to work with some of the greatest kids in the world, and many of them have gone on to be successful adults who are very much admired and respected. It makes me feel proud when I think about it, but it also makes me feel really old. Dan the man was a bass drummer in my marching band in the ninth grade. I still remember the first time he strapped on a bass drum. He could barely carry it down the street but that didn't phase him a bit. Now he's the superintendent of schools of a large public school near my home.

A shot of Dave helping a thin boy strap on a bass drum that seems way too big for him. The boy is all smiles as Dave hands him two beaters and shows him how to hit the large drum. Then a quick cut to a school board meeting. An adult version of the same boy (now balding and wearing a beard) is seated at the end of the table in a position of authority and confidently taking charge of the meeting.

His brother Mike was one of the most popular kids in band (and in the school for that matter). He was good-looking, athletic and a great student. One time in my first year there (when the kids were really acting up in band practice) Mike stepped out of the band and actually reprimanded his <u>friends</u> and <u>classmates</u> for behaving so badly. He lectured them and demanded that they treat the "new guy" with more respect. From that day on I never had a problem with discipline, and we went on to have an award winning band program there for many years. After college, Mike became the beloved and well respected principal of that school and then moved on to be the athletic director at a very large and prestigious public school.

A shot of a large marching band rehearsing in a school parking lot. The band doesn't look very sharp and the students don't appear to be giving their best effort. Several of the older boys are smiling, fooling around and talking among themselves as

they try to "test" and make life miserable for the new band director. A tall, athletic looking student holding a trumpet steps out of the band looking frustrated. He lectures his peers about their behavior and he seems to have their undivided attention. Then a quick cut to a school hallway where a confident, poised, well dressed adult version of this student smiles and respectfully answers a question from a female faculty member who approaches him with a handful of papers.

Dave's voice narrating the scene below: Lee Ann was one of my rifle twirlers in my very first marching band (the one that played for the Buffalo Bills). She loved band, worked hard and actually taught herself how to twirl a rifle. She was the cute blonde girl that all the boys had a crush on and she was fun to tease because she would whine, complain and question everything I told her to do. I just heard the other day that she's now the mayor of that town where the school is.

A shot of a cute, blonde, high school girl, proudly demonstrating to Dave that she knows how to twirl a rifle. He nods smiling with approval and gives her two thumbs up for her efforts. Not completely sure of herself yet, she drops it a couple of times and begins to pout. Dave teases her a little, but then continues to smile and encourage her until her smile comes back. Then a quick cut to a village board meeting in the local town hall. A confident, fifty year old version of the same girl (now the mayor) seems to be commanding respect, as she sits on a raised platform and supervises the meeting with authority.

Dave's voice narrating the scene below: When my son Tom was a baby and my wife brought him to our parades, I often grabbed him out of the crowd as the band passed by and marched down the street with him on my shoulders (right in the middle of my drum line). He always got a big kick out of that and seemed to love the loud pounding beat of all the drums. Tom played snare drum in my band at Lima Christian School, and was one of my worst discipline problems. Maybe because I was his dad and he knew he could get away with it, or maybe because he lost his mom in kindergarten. Now he's the father of two and a sergeant in the Army Reserve. He's got the best job in the Army, playing drums in the US Army Reserve Band. He's also in charge of PR and the recruiting of high school musicians for his army reserve band unit.

A shot of a large marching band, marching in a parade down the main street of a small town. Dave is walking proudly along on the right side of the band, smiling and waving to people in the crowd. When he spots his wife and three kids, he goes over and lifts his three-year-old son up and onto his shoulders. Carrying the dark-haired little boy he continues to march down the street with the band and moves in to march right in the middle of the drum section. Little Tom, overcome with glee, begins to smile, clap and bounce up and down to the loud pounding of the drums. A quick cut shows Dave rehearsing his marching band at Lima Christian school outdoors on a parking lot. One of the snare drummers (who looks a lot like a short haired version of Dave at that age) is fooling around, talking and smiling when he should be playing. Dave stops the band to lecture him and the boy just stares at his feet shaking his head. Another quick cut shows a very impressive looking Army Band in full dress uniform, marching in a St. Patrick's Day parade in New York City.

A wide shot shows the whole band coming toward us, then the camera continues to pan and zoom in on the drummers until it settles on a close-up of an adult version of Dave's son Tom. He is marching stone-faced with perfect posture and military bearing, playing like an accomplished professional musician.

Dave's voice narrating the scene below: Kim played bassoon, and she was already an advanced player when I took over the band program at her school. She was a little bit uppity and disrespectful toward me at first, because I wasn't her old band director and because she was the type of girl who always knew more about everything than her teachers. She teased me a lot because I didn't know all that much about the bassoon, but I tried my best to help her become a great player and a strong musician. The last I heard, she was playing in the United States Marine Corps Band. Not just one of the bands at a Marine Corps base, but THE Marine Corps Band in Washington! The presidents own band. (The one that John Philip Sousa used to conduct back in the day)

The last time I saw Kim, was when I took the band from her school, to one of her favorite annual parades a few years after she graduated. She showed up in her Marine Corps uniform, and offered to follow our band down the street in the parade, so the group behind us wouldn't get too close and spoil our music. She also decided to "stand guard" at the starting line of the judging area, so the group behind us would not play or try to enter the judging area until we had finished performing. Not many school bands have a United States Marine covering their back door in a parade. If I live to be a hundred, I'll never forget her pose that day as she stood there at attention guarding the starting line. Her military posture and body language told everyone watching or approaching that there was no way that anyone was going to get any closer to our band while she was on guard.

A shot of Dave sitting next to and talking to a tall, short haired girl with glasses holding a bassoon. She doesn't seem to be taking direction well and shakes her head as if to question or disagree with what he is telling her. In the next shot a year or two has passed and the girl is older. She smiles and nods appreciatively. She seems much more respectful now and seems to welcome Dave's instruction. She begins to play and even though we do not hear her we can tell that she is an accomplished, advanced player. Dave smiles nods and gives her a thumbs up as he listens to her playing. A quick cut shows a United States Marine Corps band in full dress uniform playing on the stage of an incredibly beautiful concert hall in Washington DC. The camera moves in on the band and as it pans through this elite group of performing musicians it settles on Kim who is one of two bassoon players. The camera pulls back to show the whole group again, then a cut to a close-up of the president, the first lady and their children, sitting in the front row enjoying the concert. Another cut then takes us to a small town parade. Dave's band is performing for the crowd and the judges in front of the reviewing stand. Far to their left, in the direction that the parade is coming from stands a lone figure in the middle of the street. It's Kim in her Marine Corps uniform, standing guard at attention just beyond the line that marks the beginning of the judging area. Looking serious & intense the scene ends with a close-up of her face.

Dave's voice narrating: Some of my former students use their musical gifts to lead worship in local churches:

A wide then close up shot of a girl playing a keyboard at the front of a church and singing into a microphone. She is part of a church worship band. The camera then switches to a close-up of the drummer and then to the young man behind the keyboard player who is playing the guitar and also singing.
We are back to a shot of Dave driving his car and smiling. He's shaking his head as he continues to talk out loud to himself about how his students have grown up and where there lives have gone.

Dave:
Well; I got to be part of the lives of some really great kids through the years. It's hard to believe they're all grown up and so many of them have done so well. Doctor's, lawyers, teachers, mayors, police officers, school superintendents, principals, military bandsmen, worship leaders, nurses, executives, pastors, parents and heads of companies.
[begins to pray]
Thank you Lord for the pride and the joy that I feel when I realize how many of my band kids have grown up to be great people who are successful and doing something worthwhile with their lives. Most of their successes have nothing to do with me being their band director, but I thank you that I could be a small part of their lives. Thank you that many of them remember me fondly and feel that band was their favorite thing in school. Thank you for the encounter with Jeremey today, (which I know did not happen by chance), and thank you that he said I was a "hero" in his eyes. Thank you for this day which was so encouraging and meaningful to me Lord. Thank you

most of all for using my gifts to help and bless so many kids, and for the powerful reminders you've given me today that my life has made a difference.

[Conclusion]

The movie is over, and the final scene is simply several short vignettes of Dave as he looks today. He is teaching, speaking, and spending time with his wife Mary, and his grandchildren. As we view these final scenes, words roll down the screen over them.

[These words roll down the screen, over the scenes below]

Dave Tripiciano, now in his sixties, still
teaches lessons and directs bands
at four Christian schools, where he
is very much loved and respected
by his students and their parents.
His band programs are also open to
and include home-schooled children.

The author of two Christian books and
the producer of eight Christian videos,
he has become a sought-after guest speaker,
traveling extensively to share
his tragic yet powerful life story.

Dave and his wife Mary, have been together
for over twenty years, and four of their
five adult children are now happily married.
He also has three beautiful grandchildren
that he loves very much and
really enjoys spending time with.

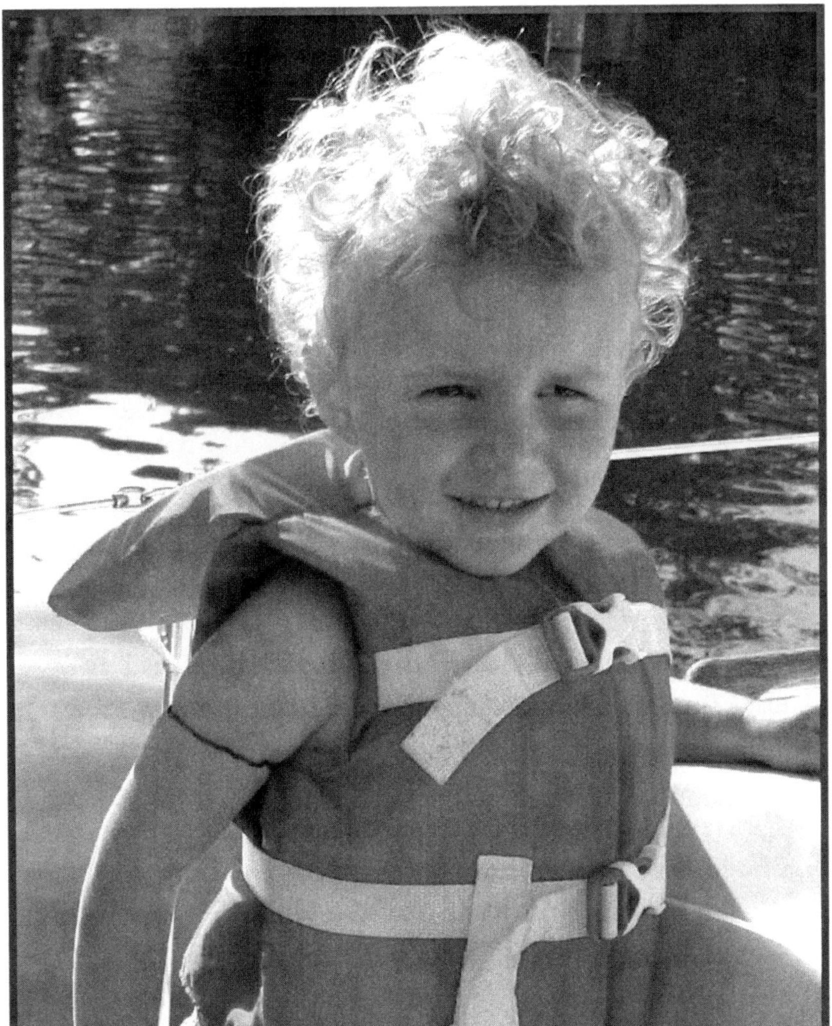

[The vignettes below are on the screen as the words roll down]

Vignette #1: Dave is seated in a chair, playing trombone with three middle school boys who are seated on both sides of him(also playing trombones). The foursome sits tall and they seem to be playing aggressively, with a lot of pride and confidence. Dave smiles as he plays. As they finish playing, he nods and smiles proudly and appears to be complimenting the boys. He gives the boy to his left a pat on the back and high-fives the others.

Vignette #2: Dave is sailing a boat alone, on a wilderness river somewhere in America.

Vignette #3: There's a large video screen at the front of a church. On the screen are striking images of trophy bucks.

Dave is standing behind the pulpit and speaking into the microphone, wearing a camouflage shirt. A close-up of his face and upper body, shows that he is speaking loudly and passionately.

Vignette #4: Dave and Mary are walking hand in hand along a village street on a beautiful summer day in the quaint small town where they live.

Vignette #5: Mary and Dave are seated comfortably on their couch in front of a cozy woodstove fire, watching TV. Dave sits on the end with his back against the arm rest. He has his arms around Mary, as she sits between his legs with her back against him.

Vignette #6: Dave plays in a tree fort with a six-year-old girl and a four-year-old boy. They are all laughing, and it's clear the children really love him.

Vignette #7: Dave pushes the six-year-old girl on a tire swing suspended from a tree while her brother watches. Both children laugh and giggle.

Vignette #8: Dave, seated in the yard in a pile of leaves, plays with the six-year-old girl, the four-year-old boy, and a tiny, one-year-old boy who is barely able to walk. He rolls in the leaves with them, tickling them mercilessly as they jump on him, wrestle with him and throw up leaves. They all laugh happily.

[**Fade to black**]

The End

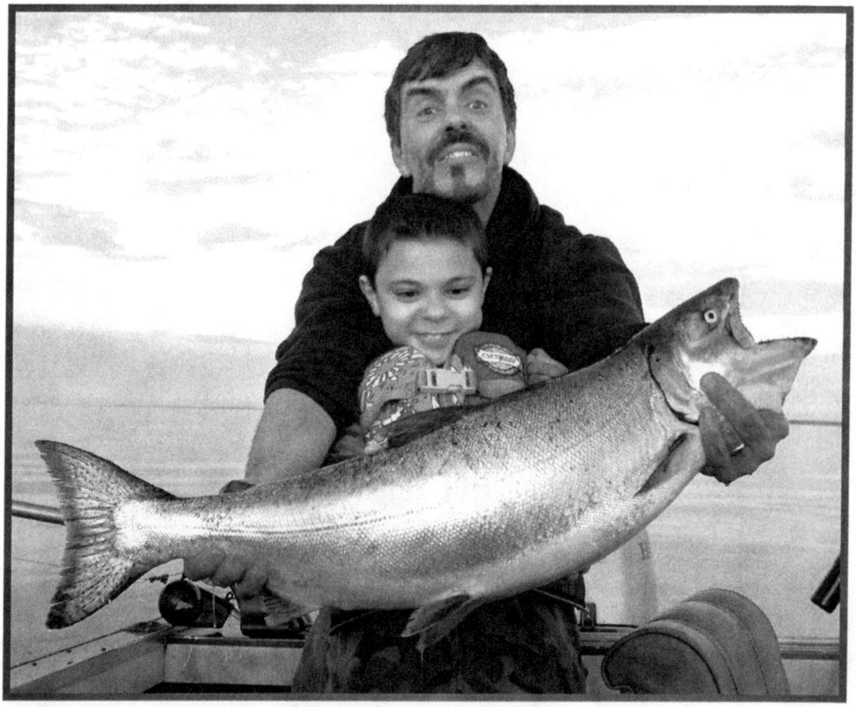

Dave Tripiciano has become a sought after guest speaker, frequently presenting hunting and wildlife seminars at outreach events. His tragic, touching story has been heard by and inspired thousands at churches across America. His life story was also dramatized and featured as an episode of the nationally syndicated Christian radio program "Unshackled" and broadcast around the world in March of 2011.

As a self centered young man, he led a life of sin and adultery as a club musician. Years later, after finding his wife dying in a wrecked car, he met and married a woman who lost her husband in a plane crash. Giving up his career as a high school band director, he began to devote his life to serving God and others. Since then he has led a life so filled with blessings, "miracles" and rewarding satisfaction; that one finds his amazing story hard to believe.

Mr. Tripiciano is a lifetime outdoorsman, sailor and the founder of "My Father's World" ministries. He is an award winning wildlife photographer, author, videographer and a New York State bow hunting instructor. In addition to his two books, he has filmed, narrated and produced eight outdoor videos which are designed for outreach and encouragement. These unique films and autographed copies of his books can be previewed, ordered, read and/or downloaded on his web site: **www.myfathersworld.com**

In addition to his outreach ministry for men, he works as a band and instrumental music teacher at four Christian schools; and also runs a band and lesson program for home schooled students. In the summer of 2012, he used his large "fixer upper" sailboat to start "**Captain Dave's Boat Cruises**" for handicapped and special needs children.